LIFE STORY
of JUDDY?

RONALD EDMUNDS

NEWMAN SPRINGS PUBLISHING
320 Broad Street
Red Bank, NJ 07701

First originally published by Newman Springs Publishing 2022

ISBN 978-1-63881-699-7 (Paperback)
ISBN 978-1-63881-700-0 (Digital)

Printed in the United States of America

To my family, whom I owe so much, with all my love.

Preface

This is my life story, from birth to age eighty. During that period, I was not accepted by my birth mother or father or by their families. I became a ward of the court, foster child to a family, someone created through incest in the genes, and child abducted from New York to California. Yet I survived and made something out of myself, going from a life of being unwanted to a life of a having a beautiful wife, four wonderful kids, eleven grandchildren, and two great grandchildren.

There are two major things that came to light in the investigation and writing of this book. In the process of being abducted from New York to California, it was clear that I needed to take care of myself and, for sure, start the process of achieving major goals that would direct my life to this day. I was old enough to understand that I would never have a real mother or father and therefore needed to protect myself.

During the writing of this book, I also better understand the true definition of *mother* and *father* and *mom* and *dad*. I have spent years thinking about those four words—*mom, dad, mother,* and *father*—and why I could make such a statement. To me, a mom or dad is someone who makes sure you have a roof over your head, clothes on your back, and food in your belly, one who is there when you are in need. A mother or father is a person who is a partner in your life, one who not only does the above but also lives your life with you. They love to do the things you love to do and are always there wanting to be part of the things you do. You put the two together, and you get a real mother and father.

I hope you enjoy reading this, and in some way, may it help you better understand you can succeed and survive in this world. God bless you.

1941

Birth Parents

Francis Edwards
1914–1987

Mary Arlene Van Gorden Edwards
1920–1983

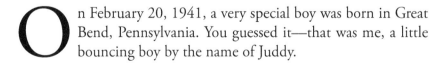

On February 20, 1941, a very special boy was born in Great Bend, Pennsylvania. You guessed it—that was me, a little bouncing boy by the name of Juddy.

It seemed that my birth mother and birth father's registered location was Broome County, New York; but for some reason, I was born in a hospital in Hallstead, Pennsylvania. The doctor was Dr. Smith of Hallstead, Pennsylvania. What a lucky doctor as he had the pleasure of bringing this cute baby into the world and starting him on the adventure of his life!

A quote that comes to my mind is from Mark Twain: "*The most important times in your life are when you are born and when you find out why.*"

How did I get my information, and why did I want to know?

A phone call in 1978, which you will read about in another chapter, made a major impact on my total life, answering the why of Mark Twain's quote. But why enter the investigation world at the age of seventy to discover who I am? Maybe you want to stop reading right now as you may find things about this person which will make you very concerned why God brought this beautiful baby boy into the world. One thing is sure: Based on the pictures, I have seen of my birth father and birth mother. I am so glad that God gave me my mother's looks.

In 2010, I began my search to find out who I am; and my wife, Mary, and I headed for Providence, Rhode Island, to investigate the man responsible for this baby boy. My half brother and his wife joined us on our voyage of discovery. In fact, they arrived before us and went to the hall of records and obtained a copy of my birth father's birth certificate.

My birth father, Francis, was born December 22, 1914. The birth certificate had the following information:

> MOTHER'S NAME: Edith, no last name
> AGE: 16
> FATHER'S NAME: None listed
> CHILD'S NAME: Frank Edwards

His name is listed as Frank Edwards on both my birth certificate and that of my full sister, Patricia. In this book, his name will be

Francis as he was called by his family, and I believe that is still what they call him.

My investigation has shown that Francis was given to Mr. and Mrs. Stanley at the time of his birth. Under rape laws and incest laws, they needed to protect his birth father because the birth mother was not the age on the birth certificate. It is believed that Mrs. Stanley, and maybe Mr. Stanley, knew the birth mother or her family. At that time, my birth father's name was changed to Howard Stanley as shown on the 1920 and 1930 census. In either 1931 or 1932, Howard Stanley (Francis Edwards) wanted to join the Civilian Conservation Corps, but it required proof of age. Gertrude Stanley, his foster mother, informed Howard Stanley that, in fact, his name was not Howard Stanley but Frank Edwards. Based on the records, I believe she explained to Frank what happened and who his birth mother and father were. She also provided documentation to prove he was Frank Edwards on the birth certificate.

At that point, my birth father understood what had taken place. He knew there were no Edwardses in his family, and I am also sure that my birth father was very aware of what had taken place. With my first DNA results, it was clear I had no Edwards in my DNA. After my half brother did his DNA test, he also had none, but we were a perfect match. I will point out that Patricia and I have different mothers from the other six siblings in Francis Edwards's family. My half brother is also a perfect match to my son William and his two sons.

Certainly this means that Patricia, my full biological sister; my half brother; and a few of my half sisters were all conceived by Francis Edwards. Because there was no mother's last name and no father's name listed on the birth certificate, it is uncertain whether Francis had any siblings. All nine of my birth father's children were born with the last name of Edwards—two were with Mary Arlene Van Gorden, and seven were with one Dorothy Moat. Out of the nine children, two were born in marriage, and one was connived. So they may never know who their birth grandmother or grandfather were. However, I discovered my biological grandfather and grandmother through my investigation.

The Stanleys did not adopt Frank, so when my half brother and I went to Rhode Island to get Francis's birth certificate, we asked for a birth certificate for "Edwards." My half brother's last name was also Edwards, and both his and Frank Edwards's names were the same on his birth certificate. Now, if he had been adopted, the records would have been sealed; and he would never have been able to receive the certificate.

Because I was later adopted and had a different last name, I had to go to court in order to obtain my original birth certificate. Only after I had proved to the court that Mr. and Mrs. Woodward, my adoptive parents, were deceased and that my birth mother and father were deceased did I receive mine. In order to get my mother's certified birth certificate, I was required to have my full sister apply for me to receive a copy. I never would have gotten it without a court case in the state of Pennsylvania.

The investigation of my birth mother, Mary Arlene Van Gorden, was a whole different process. I had located my full sister, Patricia, in 1978; and I learned a lot about Mary Van Gorden from her. She had no idea that our mother was one of twenty-one children. In fact, of her siblings, I found my cousins Ronald, Karen, Judson, Mabel, Evelyn, and Elsie—none had any idea there were that many other uncles and aunts who did not survive and who died either in the 1918 worldwide plague or in the massive flood in the late 1930s in Broome County, New York. In fact, many didn't even know about Arthur, another sibling who broke his neck falling down some steps.

Mary Arlene Van Gorden was born September 17, 1920, in Philadelphia, Pennsylvania. My birth parents, Francis and Mary, came from very different environments—one having no idea who his mother or father was, or at least not talking, and the other having a total of twenty brothers and sisters. One kind of lived a foster life, and the other experienced the death of many of her brothers and sisters. If I live long enough to get back East, one of the things on my bucket list is to go to Scranton, Pennsylvania, and Binghamton, New York, and hopefully identify the other fifteen Van Gorden children.

Based on documents that I have read, I was the second child in the marriage of Francis Edwards and Mary Arlene Edwards. Since

I was the first male born to Mary Arlene Van Gorden Edwards, I am not sure if I was named after her brother Juddy Van Gorden or her grandfather Juddy Conklin. My mother got pregnant right after turning seventeen and also without the benefit of marriage. In fact, my birth mother and birth father got married the same month that my sister, Patricia Charmaine Edwards, was born, July 26, 1938. I also believe that, because of social norms at the time, my birth mother's parents put heavy pressure on Francis Edwards to marry their daughter in order to protect her from disgrace.

Records show that the two lived together during this time in Broome County, New York. From the period of my birth until about the age of three, my life history based on relatives' stories and documents was anything but normal. At one point, my father was paying my mother to babysit both my sister and me. On another occasion, my father came home to find that the landlady was taking care of both of us because my mother was out on a date with another guy. The document tells me that, during this period in time, my birth father and birth mother were not sharing beds; but each had their own room, with my sister sleeping with my mother and me with my father.

In April of 1942, I was one year old, and documents show that my father had a problem with his mother-in-law when she left me at the hospital one day. Then he decided it was time to act and get sole custody of both my sister and me. The process started in family court with a deposition taken from my father. However, since my father was having a relationship with another woman, it was likely that, based on social norms at the time, the issue with his girlfriend might cause both my sister and me to be made wards of the court.

It is clear that the address given for my mother was not her correct address. In fact, my father knew my mother was living with her mother when she wasn't living with various gentlemen. He could have given her mother's address, and the court could have requested my mother's presence. But if my father had given the correct address and my mother had shown up, she might have dropped the bomb about my father's girlfriend. As a result, the statements in my birth father's deposition were not true. My father was awarded custody of both my sister and me, and for a period of time, we lived from place to place with him. Documents showed that his girlfriend was very unhappy to have both Patricia and me in the picture. She was very well aware that he was married, but she didn't care. He was going to be her man.

As the Second World War was taking place, my father was ordered to report for duty in December of 1942. In addition, his girlfriend was pregnant and couldn't or wouldn't take the two of us; so my father, in September of 1942, put an ad in the *Binghamton Press* newspaper for someone to care for my sister and me while he was in the service. A family by the name of Woodward came forward to care for the two of us. An agreement made between my birth dad and the Woodward family allowed them to care for my sister and me while he was in the service. He had arranged, based on records, for alimony and child support to be paid to his wife, Mary, with the understanding that a part of that money was to be given to the Woodwards. However, my mother considered the alimony to be all hers, and she did not forward any pay to the Woodwards. For sure, she had no love for my birth dad and was angry about what he had done to get custody.

In late 1942, the Woodwards notified the army that they were not receiving any monetary compensation for the care of my sister and me. The army notified my birth father, and he changed the distribution of funds. The portion that the Woodwards were to receive was then paid directly to them. But the back pay was not given to the Woodwards at that time. Having less in her alimony check each month, my birth mom and her mother headed to the Woodward home in Lisle, New York, to remove my sister and me from the Woodwards' care. The Woodwards weren't home; but Shirley Woodward, age fifteen, and Bob Woodward, age sixteen, were. Upon entering the home, my birth mom grabbed my sister, but Bob grabbed me and wouldn't allow them to have me. My birth mom and grandmother left with my sister, and I stayed with the Woodwards. I never saw my sister again until I found her many years later.

Somehow, Patricia ended up in the care of Francis's girlfriend. Francis found out from the Woodwards what had happened, and since he still had custody of Patricia, my birth mother was forced to release her. Why he didn't give her back to the Woodwards is not clear. Francis's girlfriend was pregnant with their first child. He arranged for her to receive child support for my sister, and the amount was enough to provide for the three. Army records show that he was sending the money for Patricia's care to his mother, Dorothy Edwards, of Schenectady, New York. That was not true in the records as Dorothy Edwards was not his mother but his girlfriend, Dorothy Moat; but questions would cause problems by the military in those days, plus the courts, as no relation was taking care of my sister. My investigation into the family showed that the Van Gordens were "not a good, law-abiding family." Statements made in the custody hearing stated, "We are very familiar with the Van Gordens in this court." And many other documents show similar statements. I also have a document that shows one of the children spent time in Sing Sing.

In December of 1945, Francis had served his duty in the army; and by then, his girlfriend had had a child. Since he had no desire to serve a second tour of duty, he approached the Woodwards to regain custody of me. They would not allow him to take me based on a few issues they had with him at the time. Francis then filed in family court against the Woodwards to get custody of his son. At the hearing, facts were given to the judge that caused the family court to not only question his present custody but also the custody hearing back in 1942. Francis's lies had finally caught up to him, and the hearing judge decided to make me a ward of the court and to keep me in the custody of the Woodwards. I can only assume that infidelity and Francis's perjury in the first hearing caused the judge to make me a ward of the court. At the same time, the judge tried to make my sister a ward of the court, but Francis told the court she was in Florida with her grandmother. This was not true because she was actually right in New York. When he returned home in Binghamton, New York, Francis Edward and Dorothy Moat took Pat, age eight, and put her on a Greyhound bus by herself to visit the person they called grandmother, Grandma Gertrude Stanley Jacobs.

Francis had to do three things in order to have visitations and eventually get back custody. Before there was any more discussion, Francis had to produce honest proof of these three things:

1. My birth father had to pay the Woodwards for the period of time that my mother did not provide the child-support money.
2. My birth father had to leave his girlfriend and return to his wife.
3. My birth father was to either live with his wife as a family or divorce her.

The last two reflect the social norms of the time. Also the judge ordered the Salvation Army to investigate the Woodwards. The report came back to the court very favorable to the Woodwards and included a statement that they wanted to adopt Juddy. The court allowed the Woodwards to retain custody of me until Francis Edwards met the above requirements. The judge gave very specific instructions to the Woodwards:

> Under no circumstances were the Woodwards to take me out of the state of New York without the court's permission.

For the purpose of this document, when I state Mom or Dad from this time forward, I am referring to Pauline and William Woodward. If I am referring to my birth mother or birth father, I will use the term birth mom or birth dad as they never earned the right to be called Mother and Father. Shirley and Bob are the Woodward children I grew up with, and when I was adopted at age nineteen, they then became my brother and sister.

I am afraid that, from this day forward, all children of Francis Edwards will never be able to use genealogy to trace their heritage on their father's side of their family. So all my children and all others who may have had me as their main root under the Van Gordens and

Edwards need to understand that I considered my main family the Woodwards.

As there is no DNA for Edwards, I feel sorry for six people who will never know who their grandmother and grandfather on their father's side were. Since I was raised by the Woodwards and really never got involved in this matter until I was in my late thirties, I wasn't affected, but I do feel sorry for the others. Francis and his partner, Dorothy, continued to deceive their children until the year 2010. At that time, I disclosed major findings that created some problems between members of that family and me. That was the beginning of the end for my relationship with most of the Edwards family.

I will not make any comment on my birth mom and birth dad as I wasn't present; but I can tell you, from my investigation and honest discussion with my full sister, Patricia Charmaine Edwards, they didn't even come close to being a mother or father to her. Let's not blame it all on Francis and Dorothy because Mary and her family also threw Patricia to the wind. Because no one was willing to have my sister, she was placed in the Susquehanna Home for Unwanted Children by the courts of Broome County. The interesting part is that, after she was older, my sister and her mother talked on the phone. But Mary ran off with a Mr. Hansen and really had nothing to do with Pat when she was released from the Susquehanna Home for Unwanted Children at the age of sixteen. None of Pat's family— Francis, Dorothy, and Mary Arlene—provided her with a mom and dad and, for sure, a mother and father. Only at times did Francis Edwards and his girlfriend, Dorothy Moat, provide a mom-and-dad-like true environment for her. One was a condition that caused Pat to give up a newborn that she never saw again.

The interesting game that these two played is the game of their marriage that you will read about later on. I acquired a will that shows my birth mother had two other children, a boy and a girl. I have located one of them, but I decided not to contact that one because there was no reason to open that door. They have to be in their late sixties or early seventies and have lived all these years with a mother who was theirs by the name of Mary A. Hansen. Now you have the cards I was dealt as I started my life in this world.

The Farm in Lisle, New York

1942–1946

The time from birth until this present day has had both positive and negative effects on my life. My life from September 1942 until I became of legal age was directed by the Woodwards. Based on the facts I outlined in chapter 1, many people have told me I have had a *guardian angel*.

The farm in Lisle, New York, was my first home with the Woodwards. Let me introduce them to you. These people became my foster parents and then adoptive parents, Mom and Dad.

Pauline Belle Cross Woodward
1904–1984

William Austin Woodward
1901–1994

Foster Parents and Adopted Parents

Life was great, and I was nineteen months of age as I settled down into life on the farm with the Woodwards. My sister Patricia, four and a half, arrived with me. I have to be honest: I don't remember anything from about the age of nineteen months until I was about three years of age.

Now at age eighty, I do remember a few things that took place at the age of three until we moved from the farm in 1946. Everyday events can have a lasting impact on a person, so let me try and tell you about a few that were especially memorable.

At three years of age, I started to find things to do around the farm to cause problems. I would get up each morning and think, *Well what am I going to do today?* On the farm there were no other kids my age. There were, however, two new people I will keep talking about. The Woodward family had two children much older than me—the oldest was Bob, and the other was Shirley. The funny part for them is that, for a period of about three weeks each year, they are the same age!

Each morning, it was a major issue and challenge on how I could get away with Mom thinking I had eaten all of her large breakfast. But Mom and Dad had given me a gift they were unaware of: a dog! And I wasn't going to tell them that Ruben was a gift sent from heaven and that my guardian angel was already looking out for me. And I loved that gift more each breakfast time. Since we were on the farm, Mom, Dad, Bob, Shirley, Grandma, and Grandpa ate long before I woke up. Things had to be done—milking cows at 5:00 a.m., slopping the hog, feeding the chickens, feeding the horses, and keeping all this in order. As we had forty-one cows to milk and a lot of chores to do, they started long before this kid's butt got out of bed.

The first chance of getting into trouble was me feeding Ruben under the table without Mom seeing me. I was good at it, and Ruben was like a garbage disposal. When I put my hand under the table, like a flash, the food was gone! Or if I was able to spill it off the plate, he knew just what to do, and he never gave us away. Mom always thought I was a great kid because I always cleaned my plate. I believe this ability was passed on to my daughter, Amy, as she was even better than her dad.

One day, after a great breakfast that Ruben and I had shared, we headed to the barn. When we walked out the back door, Ruben started running toward the barn. I looked up and saw Dad, Bob, and Marshall Woodward, a cousin living on the farm, pulling my friend, the big black hog, toward the regular barn from the hog pen. Ruben was going to help as he did with the cows, but Dad yelled at him to stop.

He did, but I kept running, screaming, "What are you doing to him?"

Dad told me to stop, and I did, as Ruben had done. We watched as Bob, Dad, and Marshall pulled that hog into the barn.

I looked at Ruben and said, "Let's head to the barn and see what's going on."

Then we heard the crash or, better, a sound like you hear in the sky when it is going to rain. Both Ruben and I jumped and stopped in our tracks. What happened? Then I started running toward the barn again. As I entered the barn, there on the floor was my good friend the hog, and he was dead.

Dad yelled at me and said, "I told you not to come into the barn."

Boy, did I head in the other direction! But I was crying because my good friend the hog was dead.

Soon Bob came out, took me in his arms, and told me we had to have the meat to eat. That didn't help at all because now I was going to be eating my friend. I started crying more, and Bob called for Shirley to come out to get me. I could tell Ruben wasn't upset. He just looked at me with his big brown eyes as if to say, "I'm sorry. Don't cry." What was I going to do without my afternoon napping buddy, because the hog and I always slept together for a couple of hours in the hay tunnel? Mom and Dad knew this, so why would they do this to me?

Shirley tried to turn my attention away from what had just happened, and we headed for the milk house. She had me help her put the milk from the morning milking into the milk cans. My job was to hold the cloth over the milk cans as Shirley poured the milk to strain the milk into the cans before they were picked up. Shirley showed me how to put the cloth over the new milk can so it wouldn't come lose, and she would pour the milk from one can into another to take out all the things that shouldn't be in the milk. When we filled the cans, Shirley put them in cold water until the milk truck came to take them to the dairy. We got rid of those flies and dirt that may have been in the milk pail. This was fun, and soon I forgot about what had just happened.

After Shirley and I did that job, it came back to me what had just happened to my good friend, the hog. This had been my first experience of death. My day was going to be a bummer, and I was not a very happy three-year-old troublemaker. At lunchtime, I called Ruben to join me for lunch. Shirley had made peanut butter and jelly sandwiches along with warm milk from the morning milking. The bread was nothing like what you buy at a store but bread that was made that morning; and, boy, was it good! Ruben was not that happy at lunchtime because I liked peanut butter and jelly sandwiches, and he wasn't getting any.

It was hot and humid, and Shirley suggested that we take a swim in the creek to cool off. I had no problem with that and knew Ruben would love it also. Mom and Shirley got ready to go; I just wore the clothes I had on because I would be swimming in the nude. Shirley and Mom came downstairs and grabbed some towels, and we headed down the road. The creek ran under the road, and on the other side from our house, it formed a pool.

We arrived at the pool, and Ruben just jumped in. I took my clothes off while Mom and Shirley prepared a place to put the towels. I jumped in with Ruben since it wasn't that deep, and Mom and Shirley waded into the pond for a swim. Mom was funny as she swam on her side and only a few strokes. Shirley didn't do much swimming either because there were blackberry bushes next to the pond. She was picking them and putting them in a bucket. I joined her and started picking them also, but mine weren't going in any bucket.

A few days later, I got up for another great breakfast for Ruben and myself and found that Grandma, Mom, and Shirley were very busy in the kitchen. This was not normal, so I asked Grandma what was going on. She informed me that all the neighbors were coming to our farm to harvest the crops. I asked her what's a crop, and she informed me it was time to cut the hay and corn. People started coming, not just the farmers but their wives and children too. I liked this since I had playmates my own age and didn't have to play with Ruben and chase the chickens to get into trouble. Soon all the women were working in the kitchen or outside getting the tables set up for meals. It was fun to watch, but soon we had more interesting things to do. That whole day was so much fun, and after dinner, there was a big bonfire. Grandpa sat next to the fire. If we wanted some of the corn, he got it out of the fire, peeled the husk off, rolled it in butter and on the salt block, and gave it to us. All us kids loved that as we played games and ate corn.

That evening, it was fun to chase the fireflies, but it was even more fun to pull the light off their tails and put them on our fingers as if we had rings. What a summer! One of my favorite things was in the late afternoon watching Ruben bringing in the cows as I sat with a piece of hay in my mouth.

On the cold winter nights, as the potbelly stove in the parlor was burning to provide both light and heat, Grandpa would sit in his favorite seat by the stove and start telling stories. Since he was born in 1860 during the Civil War, he had lots of war stories that his father had told him. Boy, I sure enjoyed hearing them but usually never got through them before the sleeping angel came to take me away.

One of the things I do remember was how the people, high-society people, would come near the battlefield to watch the North fight the South. In fact, we were lucky because Great-Grandpa Woodward fought at Gettysburg and was a colonel for the North and survived. In one of our visits to Gettysburg, I saw his name but never realized that was my great-grandfather.

There were other things I remember doing on the farm during that time. Each Saturday night, it was bath time. Mom produced the washtub and set it next to the wood-burning stove in the parlor. Water was brought in by the bucket from the well, heated on the wood burning stove, and then poured over me as Mother washed me.

Another was during the early spring. Dad would take the tractor and start plowing the field before planting the crops. The highlight of those days was when Dad would allow me to stand between his legs and pretend that I was really driving the tractor. Old Ruben would run alongside the tractor barking. But after a few feet, Dad had to take back the wheel if he wanted a straight line and not run over the dog.

Another time, Bob came out of the house calling my name. Now what did I do? I wasn't sure that I wanted to answer. He called me again, and when he saw me, he asked if I wanted to do something with him. That had to be better than causing trouble and spending time with the razor strap.

We headed for the tractor, and he told me to just stay there while he hooked it up to the wagon. He told me to jump in and gave Ruben the sign to also jump into the wagon. We went over to the barn, and there were grain bags with sticks in them. He placed them in the wagon along with a shovel, and we headed for the creek as Ruben was sniffing everything on the way. Bob looked at me and asked if I could help him.

When we arrived, he told Ruben and me to get out those sticks. I felt like a big guy being asked by my big brother to assist with those sticks. I am not sure how many there were because I couldn't count that high. Bob took the shovel and started digging holes by the creek. Ruben tried to help by digging next to the hole, so Bob yelled at him. Ruben just looked at him as if to say, "What's wrong?" I just sat down to watch this game between Bob and Ruben. Soon Bob and Ruben had those holes dug, and now Bob opened the grain bags and took the sticks out. Bob then asked me to help hold a stick in the middle of a hole while he threw dirt into the hole.

How stupid, I thought.

Ruben did not help put the dirt back into the hole as he had helped dig them out. When Bob finished, he told us to jump into the wagon. Ruben started running back to the barn, and so I got in by myself. Later I went back by the farm in the early 1970s, and there were those sticks grown into some very beautiful trees next to the creek. I guess Bob knew what he was doing.

In 1941, Dad got a job working for a major manufacturing company in New York, and he worked the graveyard shift. It was clear that the farm was more than he could handle, and when Bob entered the air force to go to flight school during the Second World War, Dad sold the farm and bought a house in Binghamton, New York.

What was I going to do? There were no roosters to pull feathers from, no cows, and, most of all, no Ruben. I was interested in what this new place was going to offer since the farm was all I knew. Were Grandma and Grandpa Woodward going with us?

It was an interesting time for me because the farm had been so important to me and now was being pulled out from under my feet. The good news was that I was still going to be with my family—well, at least with Mom, Dad, Grandma, and Grandpa. Bob was off to the service, and Shirley decided it was time for her to find her own place while she worked for a law firm.

1946–1949

Binghamton, New York

At five years of age, I found myself in a new home three stories high and big! And the second stage of my life began: the process of getting an education. I turned five in February, so it was my turn to enter kindergarten. Mom went with me, and we walked a long way to a funny-looking building that said "Abraham Lincoln Elementary School."

What is this? I wondered as we entered the building.

I was taken to the office where a woman was working. Mom told her I was there to enroll in kindergarten. The next thirteen years might or might not be fun, but I had no choice.

When I entered my classroom, there were a lot of kids my age! Boy, this was going to be fun, and moving to Mill Street wasn't so bad. Because my birthday was in February, I was older than many of the children in the class. The teacher asked Mom my name, and she said Juddy Edwards. The teacher took me by the hand and introduced me to the rest of the students. Then she asked me to sit next to a girl. Sitting? Why did I have to sit? I only sat when I was in trouble, so I wasn't sure what I did wrong. But the rest were sitting, so I sat down. Maybe this was the beginning of Time Out. I guess I invented it. You see, putting thumb tacks on the teacher's seat, pigtails in inkwells, and many other things caused the teachers to be very upset with me. Of course, my charm and good looks got me out of a lot of problems in those thirteen years of school.

Because my first day of school was fun and because we were living in town, maybe this life was going to be better than the farm. There, I never had kids to play with except when farmers came to help with crops or when someone showed up on the weekends to visit.

Things were going great! Mom picked me up a few times in order for me to learn my way home after school. Then I discovered many of the other kids lived in the same neighborhood, so we just all walked home together. It wasn't long before this became old hat, and I did this for the next four years.

Grandpa and Grandma Woodward were the only ones who moved with us from the farm since Bob was in the service and Shirley was living on her own and working in town. Grandma always took me into her arms and gave me a big kiss. I loved those kisses, and she seemed to understand I needed assurance that I was in good hands. Grandpa always smiled and just stared at me. It was scary when he didn't have his beard, but when he had that big white beard, he looked like Santa Claus.

I had found a few friends, and it was turning out not to be so bad. The only thing I had to remember was that, when Mom yelled for me, I'd better be in hearing distance. If I wasn't, I had a meeting with that mean razor strap.

There is a very special thing that happened while we lived in Binghamton. It was a Sunday, and many people came to our house. Some I had met, but most were new to me. Shirley came over to the house and started working with Mom to get things ready. I really wondered what was going on, and Dad informed me this was a very special day for Grandma and Grandpa. They were married sixty years on that day. I was old enough to know what marriage was about, but why celebrate? Grandma and Grandpa had five boys, and they all attended this party. A man from the newspaper was present, and they moved the couch over in front of the outside door. Mom was directing who was to sit or stand where. Sixty years of marriage, well, big deal. When do we eat that cake and ice cream?

One of the things I didn't like on the farm in New York was something that Mom had at her disposal. She had this thing you call a razor strap. I should have seen to it that it got lost prior to the move, but I didn't. The razor strap was designed to be used with a straight-edge razor to sharpen the blade when it got dull. Now this strap was used on me when I was bad, and that was the fear of my life because that razor strap and I often had the opportunity to meet each other in the bathroom just off the kitchen. I will say it was always used below the waist, but it still hurt. One time, I had done a real bad thing, so Mom told me to head to that infamous bathroom. She came in, and the next thing I knew, I was being hit by that razor strap. As I said, it was always below the waist. Well, this time I was trying to jump over it. As she swung it, I jumped and landed on a coffee can that had a very sharp edge. You guessed it: I cut the joint on my left foot, between the big toe and sole. It was a very deep cut, and I screamed. Mom understood that wasn't my normal scream and stopped. Then she saw the blood all over the bathroom floor, grabbed me, carried me to the kitchen, and got a towel. She was able to stop the bleeding, but I still have a major scar.

Bob returned from the air force as a B-17 bomber pilot after serving his three years in training and in Italy. While Bob was in the war, Mom had a nervous breakdown over the fact that Bob was in the war, and she was placed in the hospital for a while. When Bob arrived home from the war, I can still remember how big his arms looked. When we went to pick him up at the train station, he was in his military uniform. I got to ride in the back seat with him, and he allowed me to wear his air force hat. That summer, he got a job at a tar pit, and I can still remember the smell of tar that he brought into the house. He worked on this job for the summer and then headed for college in Massachusetts on the GI Bill.

Shirley moved back into the house and sometimes watched over me when Mom and Dad went someplace. Dad was able to switch from graveyard shift to day shift while we were still living in Binghamton.

Shirley was young and in love with a guy named Rudy. He would come over in the evening to be with Shirley. I created a problem for her. I wouldn't stay in my room and leave them alone, so Rudy came up with a great solution. He would pay me 5¢ to go to my room and leave them alone. Well, I didn't have a problem with that. Just keep the money coming.

Shirley and Rudy decided to get married, and did that cause a problem! Mom was not in favor of that in any way, shape, or form. Rudy was Catholic, and Mom believed that Catholics were not Christians. He was also a Democrat, and they weren't Christians either! Mom had made it very clear that we would have no part of the wedding even to the point that we would not attend the ceremony.

The day of the wedding, Mom walked out of the bedroom wearing a nice suit and told Dad and me that we were going to the wedding. Off we went to this big church, and when we entered, I knew it was a Catholic Church because I had been in one many times while walking home from school. We sat in the very back of the church. When Shirley started walking down the aisle and saw Mom and Dad, she had tears in her eyes. Shirley's uncle gave her away. As soon as the wedding was over and before they came back down the aisle, Mom made Dad and me leave because she didn't want anyone to see her there. Well, things got better after that; but one thing was for sure—Mom made it clear that, when Rudy came into our house, he was not allowed to smoke. He did honor her wishes because he knew he would otherwise not be allowed in the house.

Soon the next news arrived: Bob was coming home after graduating from college. The real news was Bob was getting married to a preacher's daughter. After the situation with Shirley, Mother couldn't have been any happier and couldn't wait for the wedding. The wedding was going to be held in the bride's church, and her father performed the ceremony.

It was a beautiful wedding, and Belle Christensen was now Belle Woodward. The time had come for Bob and Belle to head off on their honeymoon. I do remember that Bob's friends, while he and Belle were changing clothes, jacked up Bob's car in the back to put the wheels just off the ground. Bob and Belle got into the car and put it in reverse to back out of the driveway, and the back wheels just never touched the ground. They were going nowhere.

I always wondered why they went West and settled there, and one day, it came to light. Belle was pregnant at the time of the wedding. I can tell you, back in late 1940s, that was a very big no-no and, for sure, not in the most religious churches. When I found out, I never said a word to my mom.

In order to support the total family, Dad also went to work in real estate. He was a very kindhearted gentleman who did his best to support the family and allow Mom to stay home. At some point, prior to my arrival, she had been a schoolteacher. I never remember Dad getting mad at me but two times, and both times he had good cause.

With my big mouth, one day, I back talked to him in a big way. For the first time, I saw a very angry dad who was now going to use his force on my butt. I was so scared I ran into Grandma and Grandpa Woodward's bathroom to hide. There was an old cast-iron tub in the bathroom which I was able to crawl behind and wedge myself in between the wall and the tub. This bathroom was between the hallway and Grandma and Grandpa Woodward's bedroom, so it had a door into the hallway and also into the bedroom. Nobody could see me. Dad was yelling my name in such a way no pastor would have liked. I believed that, if he found me, I was dead. I stayed in that place for a long time until I was sure Dad had calmed down, and at that time, I came out. Dad wanted to know where I had been, and I showed him. Then he got his belt! No, not Mom's razor strap but Dad's belt that held his pants up.

For some reason, Mom and Dad had a brain fart to have me start accordion lessons. It was not on the top of my list! Not only that, but my first accordion teacher was a mean old woman. I would sometimes hit the wrong key on the accordion, and she would hit my right or left hand, whichever had hit the wrong key. I always took my lessons in the living room, and one time, Dad walked into the room as this old lady hit my finger with a pencil. Well, that was the end of her giving me lessons after Dad let her have it, paid her, and escorted her out the door. I still have that accordion. Why? I am not sure! Maybe because my last teacher came to Mom and Dad and told them he could not teach me anything more on the accordion. Maybe that teacher gave me encouragement that I was not just a waste and that I could really achieve something. I was also proud that Mom and Dad were proud of me. The accordion sits in our formal dining room to this day. Again, why? I am not sure.

Sometimes we had bad winter storms in New York, and as soon as the weather allowed, I got my snowsuit on with warm gloves and hat and headed outside to join the other kids in the neighborhood. Long icicles hung from the eaves of the houses, and we kids loved to break them off and pretend to have sword fights. We had a lot of fun running around getting our swords broken or running with a snow-ball to hit another icicle in order to start a war all over again.

When we had these bad storms, cars could not get up the street and could only go down. One time, I took my sled the top of the street, ran with the sled for about ten yards, jumped on the sled, and headed down that very snow-covered street. I was flying down that street! About halfway down the street, this stupid guy backed out of his driveway. I was sure he saw me, so I just kept sledding down on my American Flyer sled. I was wrong, and he kept backing out onto the street. I needed to stop my American Flyer, or I was going to get hit. Should I just roll off, or should I try and turn the sled? I chose to try and turn the sled. Sorry, too late—the car and I were going to meet. I was lucky his wife was sitting shotgun in the car because she saw me, and they stopped. Well, I still hit the car and only got a bloody nose. The woman got out of the car and hugged me tight, which put blood on her. She also grabbed some snow and put in on the back of my head while her glove stopped my bloody nose. Everything turned out okay, but again it was one of those times I was lucky or my guardian angel was watching over me. I was very lucky.

During the Second World War, our doctor's son was killed. Dr. Smith lived just across the street and a few houses down. I had been to the doctor's home a few times for scrapes and bruises since his office was in his home. Mom came to me one evening and asked if I would like to join her in going to Dr. Smith's house to pay tribute to his son. I didn't give it a thought. He was my doctor, and I liked him. So why not? We left the house, crossed the street, and arrived at Dr. Smith's home. There were people going in and going out. We stood in line while Mom talked to a lot of the people. I looked around to see how many of my friends were there and didn't see any, but so what? I was seven years of age, tall for my age, and wanted to tell my doctor I was sorry for his son's death. It took some time, but we finally were in the room where Dr. Smith stood. I was met with a total surprise. I grabbed Mom's hand and wanted to run, but I also didn't want to look chicken. I was looking at a room full of flowers, but the strange thing was that someone was lying in an open casket. I could see his nose and some of his face. I then realized he was dead and this was for people to see and pay tribute. Mom moved forward, but I stood frozen. My eyes wandered over to Dr. Smith. He saw that I was scared, so he gave me a big smile and walked over to hug me. I couldn't wait to get out of that place. I must say, each time I went to Dr. Smith's home for medical reasons, I always looked into that room hoping I wouldn't see his son in that box. If I close my eyes and think about that situation, I can still see that room and that box.

There was a very awkward moment in my early life, when I was in the third grade. I was asked by a fellow student on the playground why my mother's last name was different from mine. It was one of those situations I had never thought about.

I looked at him and said the first thing that came in my mind, "She remarried."

I know this was the first time in my life I ever gave a thought about my last name. When I got home, I asked Mom why my last name wasn't the same as hers, at which time she informed me I was not her son but she loved me like a son. Why wasn't I her son? She was Mom. Who is my mom, and why am I not with her? For some reason, I felt it was not the time to ask that question. So I kept my big mouth shut.

Mom and Dad decided to move one more time, and we were headed back to the farm environment. I had turned the great age of eight and had some farm experience. Yes, I was headed back to the farm, not as a two-year-old, but a man at the age of eight. Bring on those cows and, yes, some chickens; but I wanted Ruben.

I was looking forward to the move until I arrived there.

One look and I said, "This isn't a farm! What are we doing here? Have you lost your mind? Where are all the cows, horses, and tractors? Where is the hay and corn going to be grown?"

Dad must have lost his mind. The good news was that I could see other houses around. In fact, on each side were the types of farms we had in Lisle, New York—big ones with lots of milking cows.

1949–1954

Kirkwood, New York

Well, another move. My life has been full of moves. Don't worry. I was still with the Woodwards, and for some reason, they decided to move to a small farm in Kirkwood, New York. I believe the farming blood was just part of my dad. Plus we would be able to grow crops while having eggs and milk at a lower cost than buying them from a grocery store. This move to the county was much different from our other farm—only two acres instead of one hundred acres.

After the move, something happened that caused Mom and Dad to reach out to give assistance. The husband of a very good friend of Mother's, as well as a fellow churchwoman, were killed in an auto accident. To help out, Mom and Dad took in their son for a month or two so the family could get back to normal. He was about fourteen, and when Mom and Dad went into town, he would have me lie on the couch and pretend he was making love to me. I didn't like it but was afraid to say anything. The good news—he wasn't with us long, and he went back to be with his mother.

During this time, I was informed that we were taking in foster kids. You see, our house had five bedrooms—three upstairs and two downstairs. The one right off the kitchen was for Grandma and Grandpa Woodward. Well, being eight years of age, I was feeling like I had the whole world in my hands. I had other kids to play with, was back on the farm, and had room to roam. Dad was still working at the manufacturing plant on the day shift, plus he put a big real-estate sign on the front lawn.

Dad decided to purchase a cow, a horse, some chickens, and a couple of pigs. After my experience in Lisle on the farm, I knew what was going to happen to those pigs. I just hoped I didn't have to help.

I knew the cow required milking twice a day, and who was going to do that? It didn't take long for me to find out. Dad got the cow on a Friday, and on Saturday morning, he had me follow him to the small barn. Well, it was time for me to learn how to milk a cow. He introduced me to a milk pail and a three-legged milk stool. (By the way, I still have that crazy stool!) He showed me how to sit next to the cow. Then he had me stand up, and he told me to put one of my fingers out. He wrapped his hand around that finger, and starting at the top of my finger, he rolled his hand down to the end of my finger. He did that two or three times and then had me do that to his finger. He checked my nails and took me back to the house to cut them. We went back to the barn; and he sat down on the milk stool, took the milk pail, put it between his knees, and grabbed two of the cow's tits. Then he started the action he had shown me on my finger. Surprise! Milk came out of that thing and into the pail. Then he stopped, stood up, and motioned for me to sit down. I did as he wanted and put the big pail between my knees. Now that pail didn't want to stay there, but with pressure from my knees, it stayed. I, for the first time in my life, took ahold of those big tits with each hand and started doing what Dad had showed me. Well, guess what? With the first pull on those tits, nothing happened except the cow turned his head and looked back at me with that look, "What is going on?" After a while, I started getting milk into the pail, but I learned something else. Boy, did it hurt my wrists! The next question in my brain was how long to milk these two tits since I still had two others to do. Well, that was my first lesson on milking a cow. Do you think I let my dad know that it was too hard? No, I was eight, and I could do this. That may have been a stupid assumption. It didn't take long, however, to get the hang of it. By Monday, I was a pro. At least, I only had to feed that horse and not milk it.

How was I going to take care of these chores prior to catching the bus for school? Dad had a solution for that. Charles and Douglas, two of the three foster children, would help out. So Dad put together a schedule of who was to do what. The bad news was that he put me in charge of the chores. At the age of eight, it was my responsibility to be in charge. Thank goodness it was summer, and it was going to give me some time to get this down before we started school again.

We got up at 5:00 a.m. each day to start those chores. That stupid cow had to be milked twice a day, twelve hours after the first milking. We three learned to work together, and I became pretty good at milking that old cow. I even enjoyed squirting milk at the cats who stood around waiting for their breakfast.

During this period, Mom was always talking about dying. She was a diabetic; and Mollie Cross, her mother, had died at the age of fifty-nine as a direct result of being a diabetic. In 1948, Mom decided it was her year to die and talked about it all the time. I kept thinking, *If she dies, what happens to me?* I would have no mother and be alone again. I went upstairs to bed one night, very scared. All I could think of was the box containing Dr. Smith's son, and the more I thought about it, the more depressed and scared I became. I just broke down and started crying and crying. I went to the stairs and started shouting for Mom as I was crying. Her bedroom was downstairs, and it wasn't long before Mom came running up the stairs. She took me in her arms and asked why I was crying.

I just kept crying and said, "I don't want you to die."

I said that over and over again, and she put her arms around me and assured me she wasn't going to die. I never heard her say that she was going to die again.

Each day, I got up at 5:00 a.m. and proceeded to the barn to start my chores. One particular time, on a very cold morning, I put my hands between the cow's leg; and the warmth of her udder sure felt good. But when I did, that old cow looked back at me with a strange look, like, "Get your cold hands out of there!" I finished milking the cow and took the milk to the house. Then I remembered that I hadn't given the cow its grain—really beet pulp. I headed back to the barn and went to the grain bin. The lid on top had been broken, so Dad put a carpet over the top. I pulled it back and reached down to get the grain scoop. When I felt hair, boy, did my hand shoot back fast! I yelled for Charles and Douglas, the two foster boys, to come. Then I found a stick to move the grain scoop over in order to see what was in there. When they arrived, I took the stick and pushed the grain scoop over, but it wouldn't budge. Charles picked up the pitchfork, and I put the metal part under the scoop and flipped it. Oh, my God! It was the biggest rat I had ever seen.

Charles wanted me to stick the rat with the pitchfork, but I had a better idea. Since that rat couldn't get out of the grain bin, I wasn't scared, and I wanted to see a good fight. We had lots of cats on the farm, and they always were there when I milked. So I went looking for one certain cat, an old gray tomcat that didn't let anyone near him. I was lucky to find he was sleeping in the hay. I snuck up on him and grabbed him. He was very tense, so I tried to assure him that I wasn't going to hurt him. When we got back to Charles and Douglas at the grain bin, I lifted the cat up, took his head, and pointed down at the grain in the grain bin. Sure enough, he saw that huge rat and leaped out of my hands into the bin. It was the gladiator against the lion. Yep, we had a great time shouting and rooting as the cat and rat had the battle of their lives. We began to wonder if the rat was going to kill the cat, but that old gray tomcat didn't let us down. After he killed that heavy rat, he couldn't jump out of the grain bin with the rat in his mouth. I reached down, grabbed the tail of the rat, and lifted him out of the bin with the cat right behind jumping up as I pulled the rat up. He grabbed the rat with his paws, pulled it out of my hands, and was now going to have breakfast. The three of us shouted with joy since we had seen a great battle, and the right one won.

We found fun things to do during the cold, dark winter. One was to sit on the floor over the heat register next to our old radio to listen to *Green Hornet, Sergeant Preston,* and *Our Miss Brooks.* It was also fun to listen to other people's conversations on the phone. In those days, each family had a certain ring, like one long, two shorts, or three longs, etc. Only when it was our ring would we pick up the phone to talk to the person who called. There was a certain ring I always enjoyed picking up when the phone rang, but it wasn't our ring. I learned that a guy often called a girl on that line, and by listening to their conversation, I got my free sex-education course.

In the late 1940s, we got our first black-and-white TV. Boy, we were now big time! It allowed me to stay up really late every Saturday night with Dad to watch the *WWF.* I should say so did Charles and Douglas. I also loved *Buster Brown, Mickey Mouse Club, Lone Ranger, Amos 'n' Andy, Red Skelton,* and *Jimmy Durante.* Those shows were funny and great to watch. We weren't fighting over the shows as there were only two channels at the time. By the way, you had to get up go to the TV to change the channel.

For some reason, on Saturday nights, Dad would take us to Endwell, New York, to an auction. We were always home by 10:00 p.m. to watch *WWF* on the TV. While Dad was at the auction, we could sit on top of hay bales and watch movies that were playing in a drive-in theater while having as many hot dogs and drinks as we wanted. It was great, and the three of us loved Saturday evenings.

Living there had its highs and lows. I, for the first time, was in Little League. My coach had to pick up Charles and me since we had no way to get the practices and games. Mom and Dad never came to see a game. We only had one car, and when Dad was not working at the large manufacturing company, he was selling real estate. Charles and I did make the all-star team each year we played, which was only three years.

In 1950, Grandpa Woodward passed away. Grandma Woodward came to dinner that evening, sat next to me, and started eating dinner. She never said a word. Dad asked where Grandpa was, and she just said he wasn't feeling well and decided to just stay in bed.

As soon as dinner was over, Grandma took Dad's hand and asked him to join her in the room because Grandpa Woodward's clock needed to be wound. Dad followed her into the room, and he came out shortly after and informed us that his dad had passed away. Dad said that he had passed away before dinner, but Grandma Woodward didn't want to ruin our dinner. Grandpa was always a quiet, very patient man who spent most of his day in his room. Once in a while, he would come out to the barn but only during the summertime. He was a great man and very much a wonderful husband to Grandma. Grandpa Woodward was ninety years of age when he died.

When Charles and I became old enough to join the Boy Scouts, we had to walk two miles to an old schoolhouse to have our meeting each Thursday night. Three major things happened while in the Boy Scouts over and above getting those merit badges. Charles and I went on an overnight outdoor camping retreat in the winter. Boy, it was cold, and our scoutmaster decided to set up camp next to a creek, which made our bones feel even colder. We set up camp, which was nothing more than putting our sleeping bags on the ground, no tents. The trees were the bathroom, and our scoutmaster built a fire after we gathered all the wood. We had hot dogs and beans, and then the scoutmaster took a large rock and put it in the fire. He told us all to go find our rock. No problem, I went to the creek and got mine, as did some of the others. Our scoutmaster told us to put them in the fire, and then we put them in the bottom of our sleeping bag before we went to sleep.

"You're crazy! I am not going to set my bag on fire!" I told him.

He laughed and told me we would take them out of the fire to cool off but that the rock would maintain its heat and it would keep our feet warm all night. Charles and I weren't buying this. In the middle of the night, we were freezing and got up around 3:00 a.m. We packed up and headed home for a warm bed.

The second event that happened in the Boy Scouts was the competition of selling light bulbs. This was a contest of all Boy Scouts in the Broome County packs in Windsor, New York. If you sold the most bulbs, you got a bike. Dad had bought me a bike. But Charles didn't have one, so we got started. Charles and I found it was easy selling the light bulbs. But what we didn't realize was that, because we lived on the farm and homes were very far apart, we would have to travel much farther to sell as many or more. But it was great fun. When we got to the jamboree, we came in second to a scout who lived in Windsor, in the city where he could go house to house. While we would get one house, he would get ten. Well, the scoutmaster and friends felt so bad that we had worked so hard and didn't win that bike they bought Charles a bike anyway. Wow, we did it!

Now it was time for a real competition. Charles and I had entered the naval flag code competition where we had to communicate by flag. Each team was given the same message and answer. We had to send information using flags, as they did before Morse code, to our partner across the gym. He had to write down what was sent and then had to flag code the answer back to you. Well, we won that contest. Don't remember what we got, but we farm boys showed those city slickers we had some smarts.

Then it was Halloween on a Thursday night along with Boy Scouts night. So what do we do on this Halloween to leave our mark? After the meeting was over, we headed for home, which was about two miles of walking. We passed a big red barn on the way home every Thursday night, and as it was Halloween, we had to do something. We were tired of placing outhouses behind the hole, so as we approached the big red barn, one of the guys thought it would be fun to put a calf up on the barn roof. It didn't take us long to all agree with that wonderful idea. With that said, we proceeded to get a calf, some rope, and a large belt from the conveyor machine. The idea was to string the rope over the pulley at the top of the barn, tie the rope to the conveyor belt, and place the belt under the calf. Someone had to get on to the roof to finish putting the calf up on the roof. The others would be on the ground pulling that calf to the roof. Now the house and the barn were very close to each other. On one side of the barn, we were protected from the farmhouse, and on the other side would be right in front of the front door. As we started pulling the calf into the air, she did not like it and started mooing very loudly, which caused the farmer to open the front door and yell. With that, the calf was returned to the ground, and the people on the roof started heading toward the side of the barn where the farmer couldn't see them. One problem, I was on the roof; and with the scramble, I somehow fell off the barn roof on the wrong side. As I hit the ground, I started running. Another problem, the farmer had a shotgun loaded with rock salt. You guessed it—he shot me in the back. That didn't stop me. I just kept running, but I was in great pain. As we all crossed the field and out of range, it was time to see how bad I was hit. My back was bleeding, and rock salt was embedded in my back. The gang decided it was time to take me to the Susquehanna River and soak the rock salt out of my back and care for my wounds. Keep in mind: This was Halloween at the end of October, and the water was anything but warm. Charles went home and got me a new shirt and pants, so I finally had dry clothes. I don't believe the Woodwards ever knew, and for sure, I wasn't going to tell them. I can assure you, for about one week, I was in great pain; but when at home, I could not show any pain when in sight of the Woodwards. Just a young guy having some fun.

Oh, one other story I need to tell you. As I said, we had chickens. After a few years, Dad didn't think they were producing eggs as well as they should be, so it was then time to kill them. He handed me a meat cleaver and told me to grab one of the chickens. I had to lay its head on a wooden stump and then cut its head off. Then I tossed the rest of the chicken on the ground, and some would start running a few feet before they fell down for keeps. Charles, Douglas, and Rose Mary, their youngest sister, would go get the chickens and give them to either Mother or Shirley, as they showed up to assist. They would dunk the headless chickens into scalding-hot water so they could pull the feathers off. We sold the chickens and used the money to buy some more Rhode Island Red chickens. Oh, did the cats on the farm love those chicken heads!

By this time, I had given up the accordion since the instructor had informed Mom and Dad that he could not teach me anything more. I was able to play the "Parade of the Wooden Soldiers" and the

"The Flight of the Bumblebee." And as I said in an earlier chapter—I guess I got ahead of myself, but now you have been told twice—I was good at the accordion. But I was sure glad those one-hour practices each day were over. I guess music was just in my life because I then decided to take up the baritone horn, such a big instrument. I started taking lessons in about the fifth grade, even playing at Windsor High School! That is correct—it was a high school. But the grades were kindergarten through twelfth grade. Because the horn was too big, I could not walk home with the horn at night, so we took the school bus from home and back each day. Well, as with anything else, when I took up something, I wanted to be in total control and the best at doing it. And so the adventure began. I played in the Windsor High School Band when I was in the sixth grade.

During this period of my life, in 1954, Grandma decided she didn't want to live anymore, and thus began the ending in her life. I loved that woman with all my heart as she was a woman of love and she always protected me from Mom when Mom was mad at me. Grandma was deaf most of her life and had rheumatoid arthritis in her hands. She was as gentle as any person I have ever known. If you wanted her to hear you, then you needed to either be facing her so she could see your lips or speak to her through an old-fashioned ear horn.

One day, I went out on the back porch where Grandma Woodward was sitting in a rocking chair. Remember that mean old gray tomcat we had that no one could touch? He wanted nothing to do with people, but he was a great rat killer. Well, sleeping on Grandma's lap was that old tomcat, and her hand was resting on him so she could hear him purr. She was the only one he would come to, and they enjoyed each other. In her last days, she would only take food in bed from me. One time, as both Mom and Dad were away, she asked me to hold her bedpan as she needed to use it. From 1942 until 1954, she was my rock; she never had a bad word and always showed her love to me.

I was in the room when Grandmother Woodward died—I had to be about thirteen years of age. It was February 3, 1954, and a very cold night in Kirkwood, New York. Grandma Woodward's family had gathered as everyone was sure this would be her last day. As the evening was fast approaching, we were all summoned into Grandma's bedroom, which was just off the kitchen. I stood under Grandpa Woodward's favorite clock, looking for the first time in my life at a person who was about to die. I was thirteen years of age and scared to death but also didn't want anyone to see it because I was a man. Her sons were around the bed. Closest to her was Floyd, her oldest son. Next was Archie and his wife, Mabel, who was a nurse. Then, if I remember correctly, next was Charles and his wife, Rose. On the other side of the bedroom next to me were Mom and then Fred, Grandma's youngest son, and his wife, Margaret. My dad was not in the room, and for the first time, I believed he was not a man if he couldn't be present when his mother died. I asked Mom why. She said he could not face death, which was proven to me over the years with others in the family that died.

Clara Belle Hatch, who was born in January 1871, was about to be reunited with her husband, Clark T. Woodward, of sixty-five years. I grew strength as the evening went by when suddenly Grandma's throat gave out a big rattle.

Mabel, who was a nurse, looked at us all and said, "It is the death rattle."

I got big eyed, had no idea what a death rattle was, but then I saw Grandma take a deep breath—and that was the last one. My grandmother passed away, the one who made me feel like I was loved more than anyone else in the world. Heaven was rejoicing as a newborn had entered the kingdom of heaven.

Mom went and found Dad and told him his mother was dead. He came from his bedroom to her room, his eyes wet with tears, and I knew then his love for her was a love only a son can have for a mother. Grandma and Grandpa Woodward had lived in our house from at least 1940 until she died in 1954. I am sure none of the other four sons ever gave money to Dad to support their mother and father. From that day to this, it has had a major impact on my view of what true love really was and forever will be with me.

At the funeral home, Mom was very upset. You see, Grandma Woodward had a turkey wattle. I know that because I have one, and hers was bigger than mine. When Mom stood next to the casket, she was sure that it was not Grandma Woodward. I stood next to her and also believed it was not Grandma Woodward. I can still see me standing next to Mom and her crying so badly. I went to the end of the casket and looked down at Grandma; and sure enough, from that angle, it was Grandma Woodward. I went over and took Mom's hand and led her to the end of the casket so she could see. Boy, was she upset with the funeral home for filling in that turkey wattle!

One really scary thing happened at this time. The day after Grandma's funeral, I was moved into her room to sleep at night. At the age of thirteen, I had some problems getting used to this. In fact, at night, I had some nightmares sleeping in that room.

1954–1956

Binghamton, New York

Wow, we were going to move again! My life was full of moving; and the good news was that I didn't have to milk the cow, slop the hogs, or feed the chickens. You can't have those animals in town. Yes, Mom and Dad decided to move back into town, and I was just starting junior high. More good news was that the foster agency allowed Charles, Douglas, and Rose Mary to move back to Binghamton with us. Charles and I were in the same grade in school, and since we both were farm boys, we were not going to take any crap from those city slickers. Charles was much smaller than I and was always getting into fights. I had to come to his rescue, and we became very close. He was like the real brother I never had. Those three foster children lived with us until there came a major change in my life.

What should I tell you about Juddy who only lived two years in this house? I guess I will start by telling you about that baritone horn I took up at Windsor High. Yes, I kept playing it when we returned to Binghamton, but now I was going to West Junior High School and in the seventh grade. That was a change. Before, I had been playing the baritone at Windsor High School as a sixth grader, and the only other baritone player was a senior in high school. Now, at West Junior High, we had a very great band that met each day one hour prior to school for practice. We entered many competitions and won many of them, including many against high school bands. There were four people playing the baritone horn, one an eighth grader and the first chair. The rest of us were seventh graders, and we were new to this environment of challenging for seat position. One of the guys became my best friend, and we were always switching seats from second chair to third chair. My friend also played on the *Ted Mack and the Original Amateur Hour*, which was a major television show at the time. Also, when I was in eighth grade, I went with the other guys in the baritone section to Cornell University to perform in a competition. I am proud to say we got a blue ribbon for our performance. When we came back, the local television station had us perform on TV! That was fun!

As a ninth grader, I got a paper route in the Binghamton area. I had to get up each day around 5:00 a.m., which wasn't hard since I was used to getting up early. At least I didn't need to milk that old cow. I had to bicycle about one mile to pick up the papers and then fold all the papers and deliver them to the correct homes. Also, once a month, I had to go door-to-door to collect the money each resident owed.

On another Halloween night, being me, I needed to do something to stir up trouble. I was good at that. One of my friends' grandmother owned a doll hospital. This doll hospital was a place where you could take your doll and get it repaired. I only know this because my friend told me his grandmother owned the place. I know some of you think I sent my dolls to this place. Sorry, I never played with dolls that I can remember, except this evening. My friend's grandmother had one doll that was human size, and we decided to borrow it and have some fun. Very close to my house and the doll hospital, the intersection of Seminary Avenue and Chestnut Street was very well lit and not heavily traveled. Our group consisted of six mischievous boys—of course, Charles and me; one of the band members; the grandson of the owner of the doll hospital; and two of his friends. We had a plan, and it was very simple. We were going to lay that doll in the street, put ketchup all around, and place leaves over the body so it would look just like a human being. After setting up the scene, we hid behind the bushes to watch the fruits of our labor. It didn't go the way we had planned. A car came down the street, saw the body, and slammed on his brakes; and the car behind hit him. The only thing that saved us was the gentleman in the first car ran to the body and started trying to take care of the body when he realized it was a doll. He was very mad and stood up to throw that doll as far as he could. We were lucky. Being as stupid as we were, we never gave a thought as to how we were going to get that doll back to the doll hospital after the incident.

I then realized that, because of the accident, the police were going to be involved and we needed to get that doll. If not, the police would trace it back to the doll hospital. So I ran and grabbed the doll as the other five ran in desperation to get away from that intersection. Charles and I ran as fast as we could in a direction that was not toward our house. I had this big doll, and what was I going to do with the stupid thing? We hid it in some bushes at a house on Seminary Avenue to be picked up later. Then we headed away from that house. The plan was to walk down Seminary Avenue to Oak Street, up Oak Street to Main Street, and back to Chestnut Street. While walking on Main Street, we were greeted by a police officer, and he asked us where we were going. I told the officer we were on our way home from the movies, and thank God he never asked me what movie we saw. Anyway, he said okay, and we continued to head for our house. As we started walking up Chestnut Street, about an hour after the accident, we ran into two of the other guys. The good news was one of those guys' grandmother owned the doll hospital. Now, how were we to get that doll back where it belonged? Well, the genius I am, I came up with a plan. I had this paper route and left my house around five in the morning. It was agreed that my friend would meet me on the corner of Seminary and Chestnut at five the next morning. We met and went to where I hid that stupid doll. He took it, and I continued to do the paper route.

As I broke open the papers to get ready for my route, the first thing I saw on the front page was a picture of that car and headlines about what happened. The driver's statement about a Halloween prank was on the front page. I was quick to contact each of the guys, informed them about the paper, and told them to keep their mouths shut. The good news is that, to my knowledge, no one said a word about what happened. I am sure it was because we were all afraid we would be arrested. It didn't turn out to be so much fun after all because I feared that, if anyone found out, off to jail we'd go. My history with Halloween was not very good. I either got hurt or headed toward serious trouble. So outside of calling funeral homes on Halloween to tell them Mr. X passed away, it wasn't fun anymore. I stopped celebrating that way. Instead, I was happy with the leftovers from the candy Mom gave to the trick-or-treaters.

In the summer of 1955, Mom's father, Grandpa, passed away. I didn't see him much since he lived in Endwell, and I can't remember him ever coming to our house. I do know that, each time I saw him, he was smoking a pipe. He lived right behind Aunt Elnora, my mother's sister, in Endwell; and we always saw him on special holidays almost always at her house. It seems that, every holiday, all the family members in town would gather at Aunt Elnora and Uncle Hy's home. Grandpa was always very polite to me. He had remarried, and it was clear that Mom did not like the new wife. That could be the reason I never saw them at our house.

One thing I do remember was that Endwell Junior High was just across the street from where he lived, and for many years—how long, I am not sure—Grandpa was the crossing guard for the children. This was a big thing because the road was the main route to major manufacturing companies from Binghamton and Johnson City, and it was very busy. At his funeral, I believe most of the administration plus the teachers at Endwell Junior High attended the service.

In the fall of 1956, I was hit with a major problem that has stayed with me to this day. I can still, in my mind, see where it happened. We were standing in the dining room of our home, and I remember word for word what Mom said.

"We are moving to California, and you have a choice. You either can go with us, or you can go back to your birth father. If you want to go back to your birth father, Shirley will make the arrangements."

She asked me to give them the answer the next morning. Wow, what was this all about? Going back to my birth father? Who in the rip was he? He didn't care about me. I had lived with the Woodwards for thirteen years, never with anyone else, and I didn't even know the name of my birth father or mother. In fact, I had assumed over the years, in my brain, that Mom and Dad were my birth mom and dad. It came to me that I was never told I wasn't part of the family; and because last names were very seldom used at that age, if ever, I just assumed I was a Woodward. It was all coming back as a bad dream that my last name was Edwards and not Woodward. I just assumed they were my parents because no agency ever visited me, Mom and Dad always took me on vacations, and they moved me each time they moved. In fact, by the age of fifteen, I had been in all forty-eight states on the mainland of the United States.

A book I had read titled *Man without a Country* came to my mind. Yes, *Man without a Country*. And I remember saying, "I am a boy without a family." Why was Mom asking me such a question? Of course, I wanted to go, or didn't they want me? I was never asked this question when we moved before. Wow, now what to do? I belonged to no one. It also came to me that no one loved me. I assumed that, if they asked me if I wanted to go to California with them, they would take me. That night was a very long night. My paper route was hard as my mind was not on the route, not on anything but whether they want me or not. After getting back from the route, I told Mom I wanted to go with them. I then understood I belonged to no one, and for sure, no one loved me as *mother and father*. I needed to start looking out for myself. From that point on, I would be in control of my life because I could not trust anyone. I needed to have enough money so I could control my life. That became my mission from that day forward. I had enough sense not to ask why it was a problem if I went with them. It wasn't until years later that I learned that, even though I agreed to go with them to California, they didn't have the court's permission to take me to California. I had essentially been abducted.

I went to California with them, and I understand now that my attitude had changed. I had to do everything possible to make sure I was not kicked out of the house. I was not old enough to understand the law and that all I had to do was tell the authorities that I was fifteen and abducted from New York to California and they would go to jail. Being on guard and making sure I didn't make them mad, I was now heading into the next phase of my life.

1956–1960

San Jose, California

We left for California in November when I was fifteen years of age. When I arrived in California, my name was changed from Judson Ronald Edwards to Judson Ronald Woodward. How Mom and Dad did that, I am not sure. I suspect that Shirley may have had something to do with the process because she worked for the law firm that represented Mom and Dad at the family court hearing back in 1946. Also, when I started school, I was in the ninth grade, and Mom informed me that my last name was Woodward and to sign everything as Judson Ronald Woodward. Well, my name was changed, and life went on. At least I was still with a family and safe at the present.

Shirley and Rudy Swartz came to San Jose the next summer for a visit. One morning, Mom, Shirley, and I were in the kitchen; and for some reason, Shirley and I got into it.

She looked at Mom and said, in no uncertain terms, "Please get him out of this family and send him back where he belongs!"

Once more, I realized I was a boy without a family. Mom didn't say a thing, and I wasn't sent back. I thought, at the time, maybe they didn't have the money to do so. I left the house and just walked over to the high school. Didn't anyone love me? I cried and felt like I just wanted to die.

Well, in high school, I played football, though not a starter; and I ran the mile one year in track. Then I switched to baseball since I didn't like that mile run. I also played on the basketball team but must say I was not a starter there either. I can say I wasn't really good, just good enough to make the team. I got to play a lot during my junior year in high school, and we were 22–0 and winners of the Northern California championship. The team averaged six feet, six inches, in height; and we won most of our games by more than thirty points.

My senior year, a couple of things changed—I didn't play sports since I wanted to make money and be able to drive the Woodward family car, but I did still play the baritone horn. Back at the high school, I became the first chair on the second day and never looked back. In fact, during my junior year, the state of California had a state honor band. My band director insisted that I try out for the honor band. I wasn't really interested. But all the others in the band were pushing me, so I went to the tryouts. Well, guess what! I got first chair in the California State Honor Band and had to play a solo in Brigadoon. It was one of the many compositions we played that night in front of a packed, crowded auditorium. Mom and Dad did not attend that concert.

Then, after the state honor band, I attended a dance. There was a dance band, and one of the players was playing a valve trombone. He asked me if I would like to sit in and play. I loved it and realized that I didn't need to know the slide trombone but instead I could buy a valve and slide trombone combo and maybe play in a group. I was able to afford a valve and slide trombone, so I bought them in order to play in a dance band called the Naturals—and get paid! We played for school dances and special occasions including my senior prom at the Los Gatos Country Club.

At the Los Altos High School senior prom, we had a great treat. They had hired a well-known singer at the time to be their guest singer. Yes, we were his background music. That was a very interesting night on two fronts. First we had never played background to a singer; and second, when he wasn't singing with all the girls screaming, we played for them to dance. Well, no one was dancing, and we were going to be a dud if we didn't get them to dance. During one of our breaks, someone in the group suggested we play a polka. We all looked at him as if he was crazy, but he convinced us to do so. We went back to playing; and for the rest of the night, when Ricky wasn't singing, we played polkas. The students loved it and would only dance to those polka songs.

Neither Mom nor Dad ever knew what I was doing with the band, at least they never said a word. I was a senior in high school. On Friday or Saturday nights, I was always out with the gang, or at least I think they believed that. I kept my horn and tux at one of the guys' house and only changed at the performance place. Sometimes I didn't come home until four or five in the morning. There was a place called Popeye's in Milpitas, where we could go and jam every Friday and Saturday night after two. They charged people five dollars to get in, except us, and people who came provided their own booze. We enjoyed jamming together. People got to dance, and the owners made money. We could always count on someone offering us a drink if we wanted.

One evening, I came in, and Mom was waiting for me. She asked where I had been, and I told her with friends. We got into a discussion. I didn't like what she was saying and told her so, and then I headed for my room.

Just as I was about to open my door, Mom screamed, "You are no good! We should have never brought you to California!"

Again I was reminded that I was still a young man without a family. And this was not the only time she made that statement.

After graduating from high school, since Mom and Dad did not have the money to send me to college, I worked as a truck driver and still played in a dance band called the Naturals. I made good money. We played high school dances, San Francisco nightclubs, and other special holidays like Christmas parties. We were members of the California Musician's Union since we were required to be in order to play in some of those places.

It was a very interesting fall because I also had a room at the San Jose college. The house was being rented by four senior guys who all had served in the service and were going to college on the GI Bill. I rented a room in the house and became very good friends with one of them, Don Kelley, who worked part-time at the trucking company where I was working. This was great because the house was right across the street from the girls' dorms. The house also provided a place to go when I didn't want to be around Mom and Dad. These guys had a system every Friday afternoon around four; they sponsored a TGIF party. This building was a big two-story building on the corner, which also was right next to the administration building for San Jose State.

All five of us had our own room. I will say mine didn't have much in it—just some beer kegs and a chair. Most of the time, I went home to sleep; but on Fridays, I got to attend the parties from four o'clock until about seven o'clock.

There was one thing the guys told me right off the bat, "Make sure you have a padlock on your room. You don't need people making phone calls on your phone."

I wasn't too worried because I didn't have a phone, but I put a padlock on my door anyway.

The guys bought an old refrigerator and placed it in the dining room of this old two-story house. Each Thursday, they would buy a keg of beer and would put it in the refrigerator to keep it cold. At four o'clock, they took it out and set up for the fun. As we were right across from the girls' dorm, we allowed all college girls to get in free. You guessed it: They came out of the woodwork. You say that didn't make any sense? Why would we do that and then make the guys pay five dollars to enter? It was all the beer you could drink. The word got around fast. In fact, so fast that we were the major house on campus for parties. It got so bad that the frat houses would contact us to be sure we weren't going to have a party so they could have one. In fact, that year, we replaced Chico as the number-one party college in the nation.

Around five or six o'clock each evening, the police would show up, but the house was empty when they arrived. In those days, the college had a police academy; and we made a deal with some of the guys that, if they contacted us when the cops were coming, we would allow them to come in free when they had the time. The guys watched the police bands and had one number they called. If it rang three times and no more, we yelled police and watched those college kids run like hell.

By the way, I wasn't twenty-one yet, and the guys never told me to get lost. Those young ladies from the girls' dorm across the street wanted to be around us. As you see, the other four were very good-looking seniors and single.

Oh, could I tell you a lot of stories about those six months I was in town but will stop with this one. We had a Christmas party not knowing how many would show up, but we weren't going to have beer. Instead, we bought an old bathtub and filled it full of Red Mountain wine. Yes, we had a good crowd, and one of the young ladies decided to take a bath in that tub. That's a story for another day. Now it is time for me to enter college and start a new venture.

1960–1962

Pasadena, California

By January, I had made enough money to enter college in Pasadena, California. It was over four hundred miles away from home, and for the first time, I wasn't living with Mom and Dad since 1942.

This was interesting because I only knew about three people at the college, and they attended the church we attended in San Jose. I did not have the advantage of entering with all the rest of the freshmen, and I was very unsure of the process. Lucky for me, one of the people I knew from church took me under his wing and assisted me in getting situated in college.

I was assigned a room with another student in the east dorm, and he was a religion major. Good, just what I needed for a roommate! I enrolled with a full load of college courses and went out for the freshman baseball team. I made the team, starting at third base.

A couple of funny things did happen while I was on the team. You see, the baseball field was at Brookside Park, just across from the Rose Bowl. Each day, we had to arrange our own transportation to the field. Well, there was this pitcher on our team named Jasper De Simoni from Kansas City, Kansas. He came up with a great idea. We all pitched in and bought an old hearse—yes, one of those funeral cars. The first day on the way to practice, we lost the brakes. What a ride! Most of the trip was downhill, and we shouted for Jasper to get that hearse stopped. He used the curb to slow us down. We finally did stop, but I believe we were all very pale and scared when we arrived at practice. We got the brakes fixed and, each day, went to the field in that thing. Believe me—I wouldn't go anywhere else in that thing.

Another thing we had fun doing was with a pitching machine. It was the old-fashioned type where you had to pump up the pressure if you wanted to send the ball very far.

One day, Jasper came up with an idea. "Can we build up enough pressure to send a baseball into the Rose Bowl?"

Not sure why the coach didn't stop it, but we finally got the right pressure and had a great time shooting baseballs into the Rose Bowl. After that, whenever we had old balls, you know where they were sent.

This freshman team wasn't your normal baseball team. We were a good team and sometimes had to play a college varsity baseball team. I remember we were playing the Azusa, California, varsity baseball team since the college was just starting up. I was playing third base, and the score was a little lopsided in our favor. So I decided to have some fun. Jasper was pitching. I put my baseball glove next to my mouth and yelled over to Jasper to bean the batter. Well, the crazy dude tried it; and boy, did that cause a fight! We both got thrown out of the game. The coach made us sit out couple of games. Sounded like fun to me and Jasper.

I was batting 325 when a very strange thing happened in Santa Barbara at a game. A ball was hit to third base, and I picked it up and threw the batter out at first base. Well, guess what—my arm went with it! I had a rotator cuff injury, and that ended my baseball career.

I majored in music and joined the band, or at least some semblance of a band. This was like nothing I had played in before; it was bad. I took a whole semester of band only because it counted as three units toward my music major. I did get an A.

While playing for the band, the California Musician's Union called me. They needed a trombone player to play with a major jazz band in the Hollywood Bowl. I had no car; Tom, the same person who helped me enter college from our church has a car. Off we went to the Hollywood Bowl, and I gave him a free pass to watch. I played both Friday and Saturday nights. I then enrolled in a solfège class for music majors. Boy, was I out of my league! I had no idea what the professor was talking about and just pulled a C in the class.

I had no car, so my running around was very limited. I just went to class. I wondered if I had made a major mistake going to this college. Since I did have money and wanted to do something, I got our catcher on the baseball team and his girlfriend to take me and a date to Disneyland. Yes, and I paid for all involved. It didn't go well because my friend and his girlfriend believed guys should take things slow with a woman. This was my first and only date with that young lady, and we made out all the way down and back. This did not go over well.

The most exciting thing that first semester, besides playing baseball, was which church we were going to attend on Sunday mornings and Sunday nights. There were three major churches in Pasadena, and they all were in competition with each other for students. We chose the one that served the best breakfast and then the one that had the best supper on Sunday.

After that semester, I headed home for the summer and got a job at a newspaper company. I was just waiting for the summer to be over. One thing did happen—I was nineteen years of age, and Dad came to me and said I needed to be adopted. He wanted my permission to start the process, and I said, "Of course." Just before I went back to college in September, we went to court for me to become a real Woodward. The judge asked the Woodwards' attorney if they had tried to find my real parents, and the answer was yes and they were not able to. I knew that was a lie because Shirley knew where my birth father was since they lived in the same town. I wasn't asked anything except if I wanted to be adopted, and my answer was yes. For the first time in my life, I was a real Woodward.

I had a brother and sister, even though they were much older, and a real mom and dad. Did I feel safe or secure? Not really! I still had to be in control and needed/wanted money, and no matter what happened, I couldn't be stranded with no way of support. I had spent enough years feeling no love. Yes, the Woodwards took me in and watched out for me, but Mom said things on more than one occasion to make me question if they really loved me. It was clear they adopted me to cover child abduction because, if my legal name was something other than Woodward, too many questions could be asked. I guess the real question is, What is love? As a person to this day, I am not sure what real love is.

1961–1962

Pasadena, California

In September, I reentered college and was staying in Klassen Dorm. This time I was assigned to a room with a young man from Arizona. He had lots of money and was always running around. Because he was a sophomore and I was a second-semester freshman, we didn't spend much time around each other.

The good news is I was able to get a job at a large department-store warehouse in Los Angeles. I became friends with a guy who ended up being the best man in my wedding. He had a car and was a sophomore and a preacher's son. He was a real good guy, and he took me and two young ladies to work and back each day at a very small fee.

It was always interesting riding with him down the Pasadena Freeway because it was like riding in a road race. One time, I looked around and saw one of the young ladies in the back breathing into a paper bag while her friend was trying to assist her. She had hyperventilated. That scared Lynn, so he finally slowed it down.

Another thing I found interesting was the competition between the classes, especially between the freshman and the sophomore classes. For some reason, there was a car race, and Lynn decided to drop the transmission into low gear at the speed of about fifty miles an hour. Guess what? We dropped that transmission right in the middle of Hill Avenue in Pasadena!

Outside of getting some good grades, you would not have believed I was smart if you based it on one other thing I did. The school decided to break a Guinness World Record and put more people than anyone had ever done on a single-bed mattress. Well, this stupid guy was going to join and show how big he really was. I got on the third row of bodies, and by the time enough people were on to break the record, I could not breathe anymore and was in real trouble. In fact, I couldn't even yell for help. The good news is I didn't die, or I wouldn't be writing this book.

When I went home for Christmas, I got a surprise. My brother, Bob, who was a history professor at a college in Nampa, Idaho, had a daughter with rheumatic fever. And it was hard for Bob and his wife, Belle, to attend any functions at the college or have a night out. So Mom and Dad came up with a solution. They would buy me a car if I attended that college to assist my brother, Bob, and his family. I didn't have to think twice. A car of my own. I said yes. The car my parents had bought me was a German Borgward car. You are right—a Borgward car! I had never heard of such a thing, and it was by no means the car I was expecting. Anyway, I packed it up and headed for Nampa, Idaho. Also Mom and Dad gave me a gas credit card to use for gas the rest of the time while I was in college.

January 1962–April 1962

Nampa, Idaho

This time, I didn't need help to enter college. I had a room in the dorm but a room to myself. I signed up for twelve units in the college. Because my brother was a professor and his reputation was at stake, Juddy was going to play it by the book. Plus everyone in the school soon knew my brother was Dr. Robert Woodward.

Everything was going okay; and I had a few dates with some ladies at the college—going to church on Sunday and going bowling, things like that. I never took a young lady to any place that would not be approved by the college since I was the only one in that town with a Borgward and maybe even the whole state.

Next I had to make money, or at least I thought I did. Guess what, I figured out a way—rent my car out. I was doing well with this program and making a lot of friends in school. One day in April, a person came to my classroom and said that the vice president of the college wanted to see me. So after class, I headed to his office, and he was waiting. He asked me to take a seat and then asked me why I was at a drive-in theater on Saturday night. I looked at him and said I was not at any drive-in theater on Saturday night; I was at the student center with friends. He then told me that my car was seen going into a drive-in theater and, if it wasn't me, he wanted to know who it was. You see, movie theaters were against the college rules.

I looked him in the face and told him that was none of his business, and boy, he didn't like that. He said that, if I didn't tell him, he was going to kick me out of college.

I looked him in the eye and said, "Kick me out, but I am not going to tell you."

I asked to see Dr. Riley, the president of the college, and was told he was in Europe and wouldn't be back for a couple of weeks. So he kicked me out of the college.

I went to see my brother and told him what had happened. He couldn't believe it and went directly to the vice president's office. Bob came back and wanted me to tell him who the people were.

I said, "First off, I don't agree with the school policy about movies, and second I rented out that car to some friends and would not tell on them."

I told him it wouldn't be long before they knew what happened and, if they wanted to turn themselves in, so be it.

I was out of the college. As I was packing my things, the dean of men came to see me. He wanted me to tell him the conversation I had had with the vice president of the college. I replayed the conversation, and he told me to stay put. He was going to ask for the college review board to meet on the matter. The vice president was the chairman of that review board. To make a long story short, the vice president would not change his mind, and I headed home. The guys and their girls told me they were sorry but they were not going to confess, and I knew most of the kids at the college knew who they were.

April 1962–August 1962

San Jose, California

I packed up my things. Off I went, returning to my parents' home in San Jose. When I got home, I got a big hug from Mom and Dad to let me know that they were proud of me. I went to church the following Sunday, and the pastor was surprised to see me. Now was the time to tell him. So Mom, Dad, and I went to his office and told him the story.

When the president, Dr. Riley, got back into town, he returned my pastor's phone call. I have no idea what the conversation was, but I was informed in about a week from our meeting that I could go back to the college.

I said, "Thank you, but no thanks."

I had missed three weeks of school and embarrassed my brother and his family. I was informed that the dean of women and the dean of men had sent a letter to the president of the Pasadena college stating that I should be allowed to reenter college. I know this as I got copies of the letters.

I was able, in May of 1962, to get a job with a major computer company working in their mail room. I did go back to the Pasadena college in September of 1962, but I must tell you of an adventure I had before I left for college, with my good friends Don Johnson and Ken Daniels. They both were in San Jose; and we decided that, over the Fourth of July weekend, we were going to Yosemite National Park for the holiday. We headed to Yosemite a day early and arrived in the afternoon. We chose Camp 11 to pitch our tent. There were many people staying, and it was going to be a big holiday weekend with lots of people present.

Luck was with us as three young ladies came back from wherever they had been. Guess what, they were in the tent right next to ours. It was only polite for me to go over and introduce myself to our neighbors. It wasn't long before Don, Ken, the three ladies, and I were all talking. I came up with a great idea—I asked them if they had any food, and they told me they had not bought any yet.

I looked at them and said, "Let's make a deal. We will buy the food if you will cook it for us."

The deal was signed, sealed, and delivered.

We spent four great days with those ladies. It was a very good weekend. In those days, Yosemite had a fire fall; and the first night, we all went to see it fall. It was beautiful! Seeing the fire fall from the bottom was not enough for my young lady. She wanted to go to the top to watch it fall. Well, you guessed it. I climbed with her to the top to watch it fall, but what I didn't know was she had no fear. You see, it was all bare rock up there, and there was a ledge just outside the railings that would make a good spot to sit and see the fire fall. One small problem: It was not safe, at least that's what I thought. But she felt it was okay and crawled out on that ledge.

She looked at me and said, "Are you coming?"

My mind said no way; but my body said, "Don't be a chicken," or maybe the other way around. I am not sure. I crawled out on that ledge and looked down. We were maybe a foot from the edge, and it was straight down. This was not smart.

I said, "Why don't you sit between my legs so I can make sure you don't fall."

She agreed, and I loved that as she would fall before me.

Here I was on this mountain with a beautiful twenty-nine-year-old redhead between my legs, looking forward to this bomb fire falling down into Yosemite. We were there for maybe thirty minutes with her in a sitting position and me with both hands trying to grab onto the smooth rock we were sitting on. I then realized I would feel more secure if I wrapped my arms around this young lady, so I did. She leaned back on me waiting for the fire to start and worrying about being pushed off into the Yosemite Valley. I was still not sure about this, but I enjoyed having my arms around this hot lady. Was she scared? Hell no! Was I scared? Good thing she couldn't see my very pale white face. When they pushed the fire over the side, it was something I will never forget. It was so beautiful and took less than thirty seconds to fall from the top of the mountain in Yosemite Park to the base of that mountain. When it was over, her first objective was to get the hell off of that ledge. She pushed me back and just scrambled back over the railing. I moved a lot slower, but I was so glad I was still alive.

This young lady had a wine canvas and always had wine in the canvas, so we always had something to drink. She found a way to get a small raft to go down the river, and sure enough, we were always riding the current when we weren't sipping wine. She also wanted to go swimming in the pool just above the falls. Yes, we did.

One night, there was a scream in Camp 11. It woke all of us up, and many people rushed from the tents to see what was going on. It seemed there was a lady who slept in a sleeping bag just on the ground. She had put some kind of cold cream on her face and was awakened with a bear licking the cold cream off her face. Her scream scared the bear off. How lucky she was, and I bet she never slept outside again or at least didn't put cold cream on her face.

Don was in the naval academy, and Ken worked for the same major computer company where I was working. Don had to fly back to the East Coast for school, so Ken and I drove him to the airport. We were about two hours early, so Don wanted us to drink

Manhattans while we waited. I had no idea what those things were, but I was game for anything. Ken was driving, and he didn't drink. So why not? This was not a good idea as I liked those drinks, and after two hours, both Don and I were a little on the tipsy side. In fact, they almost wouldn't let Don on the plane; and boy, was I sorry the next morning. What a bad influence that Don was on me! He forced me to have a good time—at least I thought I was having a good time. I also was reacquainted with an old friend, the thing you are supposed to sit on and not kneel in front of it. It was time to head back to college and see what other trouble I could get into.

Sept 1962–May 1963

Pasadena, California

I reentered the Pasadena college and was rooming in the Klassen House dorm. My roommate was George Winchell, whom I had known since the Binghamton years. I was now a sophomore in college, and that is only after a few interesting things that you have had the opportunity to read in prior chapters. George did one thing that I will never forget. He stayed up all night studying for a test in the room. Then at about six in the morning, he fell asleep and missed the test!

I did have a car now and found a friend who was much older than most college students. He was in late twenties and loved to play the guitar. My friend Jim seemed to be one that cared about life and where he was heading. He was from San Diego and a great guy, but he was always very quiet. Jim and I loved to go to Hollywood on Saturday nights to the Jazz Workshop to listen to jazz and drink wine. Once in a while, Jim would join in and play the guitar. It was always fun, and on some occasions, other college guys would join us. I still, to this day, don't know two things: What happened to Jim? And because he was so handsome, why weren't the ladies all over that guy? He was the cousin of one very hot woman on the campus whom I would have loved to date, but she liked a star basketball player on the college team. In fact, they married—another hot one got away.

Also we had a couple of varsity basketball players living above us, and they were always playing loud music and throwing weights on the floor to wake us up in the night. One evening, George got even. I had brought a record player with large speakers down with me. George decided to buy a record that sent a train from one speaker to the other, original surround sound. One evening, at about three in the morning, George took one of the speakers with a broom and set it up against the ceiling and the other on the floor. He put on the train record and turned the sound up very loud and sent that train from the speaker on the floor to the speaker at the ceiling with a volume that could be heard a block away if the windows were open. It did not go over well. The large basketball players were pissed, and they came running downstairs to attack the two of us. The good thing was we lived in a quad and were able to lock our door, so they would have to break it down to get us. Also the dorm chief heard the train and came running, so we survived. I watched my back for a few weeks to be sure I lived.

Again, while working at the large department store's warehouse and because I had been a truck driver after high school graduation, they hired me to drive a forklift to unload boxcars with TVs and refrigerators. I worked from 2:00 p.m. to 8:00 p.m., Monday through Friday and all-day Saturday. I was rolling in dough. Two very interesting things happened that are worth telling. The TVs were those very big consoles—in other words, very large. And I had to place them on high shelves in the warehouse. When I placed one on the rack, I always had a person who moved the console off the pallet onto the shelf. One time, we were going to put one on the fourth shelf, which was almost to the ceiling. My helper got on the pallet, and I moved the console up toward the ceiling of the warehouse. When we got to the fourth shelf, my helper moved onto the shelf and started moving the console to the shelf. But he lost control, and that thing came crashing down four stories to the concrete floor. The supervisor came over, told us to put it back on a pallet, and stuck a sticker on it which stated, "Broken in transit." Railroad's problem, not store's problem.

One other thing which I loved was a contest on Saturday. They wanted to know which driver could back up the most flatbed trailers. One was easy; two were really a challenge. But I was able to do three. Don't ask me how—just did it once and won the king of the hill.

When I went home for Christmas, I was at a store shopping for a Christmas gift for Mom when I met and fell big-time for a young lady. She had a one-year-old daughter and was a swimmer on the Santa Clara Swim Club. She held the world record for the relay team in one-by-four-hundred relay events. At least two of those swimmers on that relay team had won gold medals in the Olympics.

She lived in San Jose, and I was in Pasadena. So the road between the two cities was busy both ways each weekend. I would go there one weekend, and she would come down the next. From Christmas until school was out, we were a pair. It came to an end that summer. I arrived home for the weekend earlier than I was supposed, and when I entered her apartment, I was a little bit surprised to find her in bed with her brother's best friend. It was clear that this relationship needed to end, and that did happen. I also knew that the young man was around sixteen years of age because I knew him and her brother.

I left, and the relationship was over. She had been going to my parents' church, which was my home church. One afternoon, I got a call from the minister of the church, and he said he needed to meet with me. I asked what about and was informed it had to do with the young lady. I had a pretty good idea what it was about, and I decided I needed to have this meeting with Mom and Dad. So it was set up. At the meeting, I was informed that she was pregnant, and she was saying I was the father. I didn't say a word at the time, but I was sure I wasn't. I asked to meet with the pastor in private and told him what I found upon coming home for a visit. In addition, I hadn't been with her for over a month prior to that as it was the end of the school year and I couldn't make it.

About a month later, he informed me, Mom, and Dad that she was sure I wasn't the father.

September 1963–January 1964

Hill Street, Pasadena

In September, I went back to college, and I wasn't staying in any dorm. I got an apartment with a guy named Nate. I didn't know Nate, but we both needed to be off campus so we were free to spread our wings. Nate and I started dating girls from other colleges; and I found out real soon that, when Nate had too much to drink, it was very dangerous. You see, Nate was a weightlifter and good sized. In a pub, more than once, we found being asked to leave pub.

Nate had a great car that was his pride, and the girls were attracted to it. One night, we went to the Rose Bowl to watch a high school football game. We parked that beautiful car at the end of a street, right at the end of the hill and at an intersection. When the game was over, we came to the car to find out someone had smashed in the back of his car. It was totaled, but there was no one around, plus no note. End of his car until the insurance company settled with his father, and now we were two in a Borgward.

I do have to say one more thing. Yes, Halloween was upon us; and as a guy full of piss and vinegar, I had been looking at the street called Breese Avenue. It was about one-fourth mile long and ended at the entrance of the college. On each side of the street were large palm trees, and of course, the trunks went way up in the air before you found any palm. So in my demented mind, I got a bunch of guys with the same mindset to go with me. We each got a coffee can full of gas, and each had a tree. As we didn't have enough guys, we had to do every other one, back and forth across the street. There weren't that many demented guys at that time, and women can't keep their mouths shut. We had a car at the top of a hill next to the college, so when those trees were set ablaze, we could get out of there fast. You guessed it: We set them on fire and had a place we could go to watch. What a blaze! It lit up the whole street, and people came running out of their houses. Soon the fire department arrived. I believe the statute of limitation has long since passed, so I am revealing what this demented guy did that Halloween. If the limitation hasn't passed, the prisons have free meals, free medical, and lots of people to interact with. Just another fun Halloween. I don't do that anymore—too old. Just eat the candy that kids don't collect from our house.

Party time was the rule. Yes, I was working at the Broadway and had money. Plus I found out the federal government had a grant program which allowed me to borrow money for my school tuition. We did make a few trips to Mexico, which, in those days, was safe. In fact, we made a little extra money doing this. Guys wanted to get their cars' interiors tuck and rolled, and it was cheap to do in Mexico. We figured out that, if we stayed to watch or if we gave some good booze to the workers, we got the tuck and roll done with new fishing line. If we left, the job was done with old fishing line used by fishermen. After a couple of weeks, it really stunk, and we had a mess. The word got around that we could guarantee new fishline, and we were asked to assist in the work done to friends' cars in Mexico. We used one shop where they knew us, and we made sure they had the best booze. And we received a fee for our services.

One thing that was probably the funniest thing while Nate and I lived together involved a large bell the college had that they rang upon winning a basketball game. At one particular game, the college was playing a team in Santa Barbara, and the bell was there with the students. The word had gotten around the league about this bell, and at Santa Barbara, a group of their students decided to kidnap that bell. As no one was watching over the bell from the college, it was an easy task. We won that game, and when they went to get the bell out of the school van, it was gone. Nate and I had gone to the game, and the president of the student body came to us and asked if we could find the bell. We weren't in the mainstream of the student body; and therefore, if we nosed around, no one would believe we were guys from the other college.

When asked, we looked at the student body president and laughed. "We are not good enough to be part of this student body, but when you are in trouble, you come running. Why should we help you out?"

But for some reason, we said okay and started the process of doing the investigation in a very quiet way. Since we were a couple of guys that, for sure, were not from a religious college, we got the trust of some of the Santa Barbara students because they believed we were on their side. After a bit of "guy talk," we found out where that bell was: at the end of the Santa Barbara pier! In other words, the ocean had a metal meal. For some reason, we decided not to tell the student body president that night or the next week. We kept telling him we were still investigating. When we did tell him where it was, the students looked at us in a new light. All of a sudden, we became friends with the student body president and other leaders of the campus.

This relationship was not working out well. I could tell you more stories about the things that Nate and I did, but I will tell you that the dean of men of the college came over to our apartment wanting to search our apartment. We asked him if he had a search warrant, and he tried to tell us that the college had the right to search anytime it wanted. We sent him on his way; and he realized that, if he pushed it, he was going to be physically thrown out. We got called in the next day by the dean of students and were warned that he was watching us. Good news, we now knew we had made the dean's list!

During this time, I got the opportunity to drive a float in the New Year's Day parade, which wasn't as great as it sounds. We had to be at the parade site at midnight and stay until we drove the float, which didn't start until 8:00 a.m. That was to make sure of two things—they had the correct number of drivers and that you were sober. I remember sitting on this seat with a steering wheel in my hand, but I couldn't see a thing. Another person was up front lying down and telling me when to stop and when to go, and he had to make sure we followed the marked line for the parade. I got through it and never had a desire to do that again.

While living with Nate, I was playing around too much and having too much fun on the weekends. I was put on probation at college for grades and had to pick up my grade point average the next semester in order to stay.

January 1964–May 1964

Los Robles, Pasadena

In January, Nate and I agreed to separate. Why? I am not sure now, but he moved in with another guy he knew before me, and I got an apartment with Joe and Ron in Pasadena.

Yes, I moved again. This time, I had a three-bedroom apartment with two other roommates. Ron was a senior in college, and Joe was a junior like me. We now had an apartment that had a swimming pool and lots of good-looking young ladies. We were close to the college but far enough away that the school wasn't looking over our shoulder. I also was on probation for my low grades, so I needed to get my act together and get some grades. This semester was going to be one that I just took classes that allowed me to pull those grades up. It was somewhat a waste from the standpoint of my major to graduate. I took two business classes, Introduction to Accounting, Business Law, Beginning Tennis, Basketball, and Band. That was a total of twelve units, and I got a B in both Introduction to Accounting and Business Law and A in the other three, which got me off probation.

The two people I roomed with were not partygoers but students with a future in mind. Ron was premed, and I knew him from our church in San Jose. Ron introduced me to Joe, who was working on a business degree to become a CPA. Joe worked in the evenings at Orthopedics Hospital in Los Angeles in payroll, and Ron studied all the time.

That fall, I became very good friends with three of the varsity basketball players—Lloyd, John, and Ben. In fact, that relationship lasted through the rest of my college career. All three of the guys were African Americans and the only ones in the college.

Lloyd came to me one day because of my Borgward. Now I have to say no one had ever seen one, and since it was a European car, people believed I was rich and the car cost a lot of money. Lloyd asked if I would be willing to take him and his girlfriend to the Saturday-night Black frat basketball league at a college in Los Angeles. I told him sure and I would love to. On that day, we headed to pick up his girlfriend in Los Angeles. After we picked her up, they informed me that there was another person I needed to pick up, a friend of his girlfriend, and she wanted to go. I asked for directions and found myself in Beverly Hills in the rich section. We pulled up outside her home, and Lloyd asked me if I would go up and get her. So I walked up to the door and knocked, and when the door opened, there stood a very well-dressed African American gentleman. I told him I was there to pick up his daughter. Lloyd had told me her name, but I couldn't remember it. The man called his daughter, and she came, a very attractive young lady. We headed for the car, and I opened her door for her. She got herself comfortable while I went around the car. When I opened the door, I found her sitting very close to the driver's seat. Yep, I was on a blind date. In fact, a date I didn't even know about! And she was going to sit right next to me. Off we went. When we arrived at the game, we got out of the car, and she took my hand. When we entered the gym, I bet there were maybe five people who were White in that gym, and three of them were referees. The gym was packed, and I could feel the hair on the back of my neck rise as I felt like the total crowd was looking at me. Well, I had a great night; but when Lloyd and I were alone, we had a conversation.

One day, Ron told me about a young lady, Mary, at the college whom he was going to ask out. I asked him to point her out to me when we were on campus, and he did. I laughed and told him no way was she going out with him. I was acting so smart that I told him I could take her out.

At that point, he said, "No way"; and we made a bet.

Now the challenge was on me. How was I going to get her to go out with me with my reputation on campus? I had to put a plan together. I was talking to my friend Lynn, whom I had worked with at the Broadway warehouse. Lynn asked me to point out the young lady, which I did. He told me that his wife worked with her. With that information, I had an idea, and now was the time to sell Lynn on having his wife arrange a double date with her and that I would pay for dinner. Lynn and his wife, Carol, were still in college and had little money to spend on things like going out to dinner; so Lynn said he would see what he could do.

A couple of days later, Lynn came back and said Carol would do it, but I had to ask Mary. So then, I had to build up my courage to ask her out. The first thing was to introduce myself and then go for the touchdown. To make a long story short, I told her I knew Lynn and Carol, wanted to take them out to dinner, and wondered if she would be willing to be my date. I didn't get a yes or no, but she would think about it.

I contacted Lynn and had Carol talk to Mary so she would know for sure I was telling the truth and that I was really a nice guy. With Carol's sales job, the date was set up for the dinner date. I took the three of them to dinner at a very nice restaurant, the Peppermill in Pasadena. The date was a bust. I did not like her, and for sure, she didn't like me. She was a religious young lady, and I was a man of the world. Anyway, I did win the bet, which covered my expenses.

This semester was very interesting, but not much happened. We mostly just studied, but I did take another young lady from the college out. I am not sure why, but I guess I just wanted to see if another young lady would go out with me. I chose one that was hot and in the right college group. To my surprise, she accepted, and I took her to Hollywood for dinner. We spent some time at the Jazz Workshop on Sunset Drive. It was a pleasant date but just one of those where I wanted to prove something and did. I never called her again and, in fact, didn't even talk to her after that date. Oh, I did kiss her good night; I had to see if she would do that. Yes, we sucked face.

Ron, Joe, and I spent the summer at the apartment; and I wasn't sure if I was working or not. But Ron got accepted at dental college, and off he went in August to Chicago to start a new adventure. I could tell you a few other things that summer, but in order for this not to be X-rated, I will just leave it alone. It was a very hot summer with all those wonderful, beautiful women around the pool, if you get what I mean.

Fall classes began, and Joe and I were still in the same apartment. It was my junior year, and I signed up for a life science class. When I went to the class, the professor asked us to sit in alphabetical order. As it was a theater-type setting, I was sitting next to last in the back and behind a young lady who was very hot. I hit the guy next to me and told him I was going to take her out. I did not recognize the young lady. As I was telling the guy next to me, the professor, who was maybe a year older than I, started having words with that young lady in front of me about being quiet.

After he finished his stupid remarks to show he was important and in charge, I said, "Sir, you have the wrong person. It was me talking, and you need to give that young lady an apology."

Well, it was clear he didn't like that, and now I was on the bad side of that professor. Did I care? No. He put his pants on the same way I did, or at least I assumed he did, one leg at a time.

So after class, I made my move, only to find out this was Mary, the young lady I had taken out on a bet in the spring. This was not good, but for some reason, I still wanted to be with her and started asking her out. With my reputation, the memory of the prior date, and my comment to the professor, the answer was no. I wasn't going to take that as an answer; I guess because nothing good ever comes easy.

Over the next few months, I tried and tried and tried with the same result. I guess I was finally thinking about whom I might live the rest of my life with. In my mind, I had three young ladies from the college whom I believed I would like to be with and maybe marry. So with that in mind, Mary was first on the list, and off I went to find out. I was working at a store's warehouse driving forklift and somehow arranged to have a Friday night off. I decided I wanted to go the college basketball game in Redlands. I called Mary and asked if she would be willing to attend the basketball game with me. To my surprise, she said yes, and was I excited!

After hanging up, I realized I had screwed up. The game was on a Friday night at Redlands; and I had no money for gas, food, or tickets. And I didn't get paid until Monday. My roommate and friends were pushing me to ask her to pay our way, and then I would pay her back on Tuesday after I got paid. I asked her. The answer was no, and my date was over. I wanted to go to that game but had no money. Living in an apartment complex, there were a couple of very attractive young ladies who lived by the pool. Both worked at a department store in Pasadena, in the cosmetics department. So we were talking, and I said I would really like to go to that basketball game but had no money until Monday. One of the young ladies told me she would pay and go with me. For your information, I did pay her back the next Tuesday—the gas, the food, and the cost of the game.

You guessed it: As the two of us entered the gym, the first person to see us was Mary, whom I had asked first. I could tell by her look that I had come up with a reason to get rid of her so I could take this good-looking blonde to the game. Well, for sure, I had messed that up; but my desire was still to take Mary out. So with the ability to never quit, I started those phone calls again. Yes, you know the answer—I was not getting anywhere. In fact, in December, our college played in a Christmas basketball tournament in Chico, California. Mary lived in Red Bluff, which was about a forty-minute drive. I told her I would see her at the game. I didn't get a yes or no, but I had the impression it was a pretty good chance she would come. Her dad was a basketball nut and loved the college. I talked my good friend Don Kelly into coming with me, and we drove from San Jose to Chico in order to see the game. Mary didn't show up, and boy, did I get a kidding from my friend.

January 1965–May 1965

Monterey Park, California

In the first part of January, Joe and I decided to leave our apartment in Pasadena and move to Monterey Park. That put us far enough away so the school would have no idea what we were doing. So off we moved to Monterey Park for a new start.

I informed Joe I was going to make one more phone call to ask Mary out, and if she said no, it was time to move on to the other two ladies before they got away. I made that phone call; and when I asked her to go to church with me, this time, I got a yes. The rest of the story is history because we have been married for fifty-five years and have four wonderful children, eleven terrific grandchildren, and two great-grandchildren. I will point out that, after that date, church once more became very important to me. It was very important to her and allowed me to keep dating her. More about that later.

I worked at some interesting jobs during the first part of that semester. I had a job coaching PE at a private school. Because I kidded too much with the kids, I got fired. I then I took a job at an ice-cream parlor on Colorado Boulevard in Pasadena. By then, I was in love and wanted to ask Mary to marry me. The question was how to afford an engagement ring. Sell my trombone! I put an ad in the paper, and sure enough, a person came and bought it.

As was the practice, you needed to ask the young lady's father for her hand in marriage. One Sunday evening, we had gone to a church in Anaheim, and the pastor there had been my former pastor in San Jose. Mary was wearing the engagement ring, and he saw we were engaged. He announced it in church, so now the secret was out. Other students from the college were also in church, so that night, I had to call her father to ask for her hand in marriage. We had planned on doing it at Easter when we went to her home. Back in Pasadena, outside the ice-cream shop where I worked, on a pay phone, I made that call to ask her father for his daughter's hand in marriage. He was entertaining guests; so I talked to her mother who responded, no, she was too young and, no, I couldn't marry her. With that, I handed the phone to Mary, and she believed her mother had said yes. Somehow Mary convinced her mother she loved me and was going to marry me.

Now, when people ask me where my trombone is, I point to Mary's heart-shaped necklace, which has the original diamond embedded in it. Many years later, we purchased matching rings with one exception—Mary's has a large diamond on top of hers. They were designed by a jeweler in Chicago when we lived there.

Soon after that, I decided I didn't want to work at the ice-cream shop anymore and had no job. I was still living in Monterey Park, and I told Joe I had to get a job. To my surprise, he informed me that they needed a ward clerk at the director of nursing office of the hospital where he worked. I applied and got the job, so now I was working the 3:00 p.m. to 11:30 p.m. shift, forty hours a week, and taking a full load at the college. I also had evening duty in the morgue for when people died in the hospital or accidents happened on the Harbor Freeway, which was located just outside of the hospital. I could write a whole book just telling you about my morgue experiences, but I will spare you that news. I will say it was quiet and I had a cold place for my lunch. If I went to get my lunch and it wasn't there, I knew that person wasn't dead. I soon learned two things: One, if the floor called that someone had died, I waited for over an hour to go up and get the body. Two, when doctors did autopsies and didn't clean up and put parts back, I had to do that. Sewing was not my major, and boy, did some look bad. I will point out I was still in college and doing very well with my grades. I wasn't setting the world on fire but good enough that I didn't get put back on probation.

I spent most of my time with Mary as we were trying to decide when would be a great time to get married. We did go to her parents, and I can tell you my reception was with open arms. In fact, her brother Gary did his best to get me in trouble with my future mother-in-law. He asked me if I would like to shoot canning jars, and I said why not. We went to the shed with Dad's old gun and took about a dozen jars. The objective was to throw them into the Sacramento River and try to break them with your shot. Well, I didn't have a problem hitting them, but Gary did. I broke everyone I shot at when, all of a sudden, Mom came out asked us what we were doing. We told her we were just having fun. Was she upset!

And all Gary said was "I didn't break them. Juddy did!"

Bad way to get your future mother-in-law to like you, let alone love you.

When school was out for the summer, we picked a date for the wedding, August 14, 1965. Mary stayed at school, and we took a US history class together in summer school before she had to go home to finish planning the wedding. I was working at the hospital, so we got an apartment in Pasadena where I lived by myself until we got married.

June 1965–January 1966

Pasadena, California

Mary and I were married on August 14, 1965, and we went on our honeymoon to Fort Bragg, California. I felt a little cheap and promised her that, on our tenth wedding anniversary, I would take her anywhere in the world she wanted to go.

We were married in Santa Cruz, California, and my best man (the same guy that we went on our first date with) screwed up. He had relatives living in Santa Cruz, so he arranged for me to park my car there. He would pick me up, and we'd go to the church together. That was all okay, but I had given him the marriage license. When he came over to pick me up, there was one problem—he didn't bring the license with him; and I am sure, looking back, that was on purpose. At the end of the wedding ceremony, the pastor asked for the wedding license, and I looked at Lynn. He searched his pockets, but no wedding license. I am not sure I believed the next part, but he told me he forgot it and would have to go get it. The problem was he took the singer for the wedding with him, who was also from the college.

They came back with the license, and we had a great reception that evening. We changed our clothes, and it came time to head to our car. Lynn drove us to his relative's place; and when we got there, Mary's father, brother, and many people from college were parked waiting for us. We got out of Lynn's car and went to get into our Ford—yes, not the Borgward. We were given a car by my parents for our wedding present, and they traded in the Borgward.

As I opened the door of the car, there was a smell that I will never forget. Someone had poured a whole bottle of cheap perfume in the car. And there were all kinds of writings on the windows of the car. People later told me Mary's dad wrote most of them. The one I still remember was the one on the windshield, which said "HOT SPRINGS in the OLD TOWN TONIGHT."

I started the car and knew I didn't want to go the hotel because I didn't know who might have been following us and what would happen. Off we went with the intent of losing them. It wasn't long before we realized that something else had been done. They put Limburger cheese on the engine, and the smell was something that no one wants to have in a car—at least not until they have babies. Based on all the writing on the windshield, we were having trouble seeing. I lost the followers and found a gas station with a water hose.

We stopped and were cleaning the window when someone yelled, "There they are!"

You guessed it: Those guys had found us, and the chase was on again. The leader of the gang was Auburn, Mary's father.

We finally got rid of them and were in our room for our first night of marriage. This was the first time I could make love to the woman whom I had fallen in love with. It was for sure an interesting night, but I will leave it at that.

The next morning, before we headed up north, we needed to spend some time getting the smell out of the car and engine. We also needed to clean up the sides since we didn't need everyone from Santa Cruz to Fort Bragg knowing we just got married.

Mary insisted that we go up Route 1 from San Francisco to Fort Bragg. Being a well-behaved husband with my chance to please her, I did just that. I also learned something about my new wife real fast. We had no sooner gotten on Highway 1 with the beautiful Pacific Ocean view when I looked over and found Mary sound asleep. I guess I kept her up too late the night before. I should be ashamed of myself. To this day, she has not changed. When we start traveling in the car, she is going to sleep.

After a few days, we left Fort Bragg and drove down to Pasadena to settle into our apartment and get ready for the next semester of college. I was going to be a senior, and I only had one week of paid vacation from the hospital. When we returned back to Pasadena, our singer at the wedding, one of those wise guys, and his wife had tickets to a Dodger baseball game. It was a doubleheader, and we joined them, which made for a wonderful evening with lots of talk about the exciting evening after the wedding and that famous chase. I did learn a lot about my father-in-law, the one who wouldn't even speak to me the first time Mary and I rode in his car from Pasadena to Redlands for a basketball game and back.

Good thing the apartment was furnished since we had no furniture and no TV. So our first major purchase as a married couple was to go into debt for that color TV. I was married and in debt with something besides a college bill. My lifestyle had to change.

Going grocery shopping for the first time, I realized, *This woman is born to shop.*

I have learned to live with that for fifty-five years.

We moved into our apartment together around the third week in August even though we had rented it starting the first of August. We were married and in our apartment as husband and wife, and school was going to start soon. I also had to get back to work at the hospital. This was during the time of the Watts Riots in Los Angeles, and the hospital was located just outside of Watts. For those people who may not know what the Watts Riots were, it was a movement by the African Americans in Los Angeles with burnings and killings to show that they were tired of the conditions, lack of equal rights, and police brutality. They were going to destroy their own community to show their displeasure with their life's conditions.

The first night I showed up for work, we had the National Guard around the building. I must say that, by the time I went back to work, the government had the rioting mostly under control. I am sure what I just said is the same problem we have today; things haven't changed much.

Mary entered college for her junior year, and I was in my senior year. We had two cars because she had her grandmother's old car. She got a job at an insurance company in Pasadena, and I had the job at the hospital. We didn't ride together since she went one direction to work and I went another. She worked one to five in the afternoon, and you know my shift. We both were busy with school while the Vietnam War was going on, but I had a student deferment. No worry. In December, the federal government changed the rules. One needed to be married and a student for a deferment. Since I was married, I filed for another deferment as a married student, which was approved.

Then we decided to move out of the apartment. Some of Mary's relatives were going to provide us with furniture to start our life together. We found a very small home in Pasadena, about three blocks from the college. Because of what had happened before, I wanted to live as far away from the college as possible, and now I wanted to live close by. I had gotten married and become a Christian, and church was becoming very important to me.

January 1966–May 1966

Pasadena, California

Sometime in early 1966, the federal government changed the student deferment rules again, and you could only have a student deferment if you were married and had a family. Mary was pregnant at that time, and therefore, I got another student deferment and was able to graduate from college without having to serve in the military.

Our home was very interesting. We got our first dog named Little Ollie, a miniature dachshund. We had a three-fourth rollout bed, and her aunt asked us to take care of their full-sized poodle for a weekend. There we were, Mary and I, in bed. She was pregnant, a small dog under the covers at the bottom of our feet, and that big poodle on top of the covers. What a life! Mary completed the spring semester, but because the baby was due in October, she decided to work full-time at the insurance company as long as they would allow her. When I had days off, we had lots of friends and church functions to attend. When I was working, Mary's college roommates would stop by and keep her company.

Graduation time came. I had a wife with a very large belly, but I was so proud I was really, finally going to graduate! Not sure I would have if it wasn't for Mary. You see, I hated English, which I took the first semester of my freshman year and again the last semester of my senior year. It is a good thing Mary was able to assist me to get through that stupid course. Present at the graduation ceremony were Mary, her parents, and her brother. My mom and dad were not able to make it to the graduation. I felt bad, but I also had a wonderful wife with me and a child on the way. I graduated and was glad to be out of school. I still had the job at the hospital, which allowed me to look for a real job during the day.

1966–1967

El Monte, California

After graduation, we moved to El Monte, California. I was working for an insurance company in West Covina, California. I guess they hired me because of my work at the hospital in Los Angeles. They thought I might make a good bodily injury claims adjuster because of my experience there. The bad news was I was going to have to take some classes at the law school at Stanford University in Palo Alto. I was going to have to leave my beautiful wife while she had a big belly, and she was due in October. Off I went to Stanford University where the classes were five days a week from 7:00 a.m. to 5:00 p.m. One class was tort law. I learned to investigate accidents, take depositions, review medical records, and represent the insurance company at special arbitrations and special pretrials.

Mary was able to visit me one weekend, but we were apart for the first time in our marriage. I was not happy about this, but the real world causes you to have to do things that you may not want to do.

You know in the long run it will be best for your family. Soon I was going to be responsible for three people, and I needed to put my nose to the book, attend the school, and make a good income for my family. After the school, which I passed with honors, I started working in the claims adjuster's office in West Covina and had a company car.

The baby's arrival began early in the morning, and Mary tapped me and said, "Wake up! My water broke!"

I became aware that she was trying to tell me something. Not sure I really understood what water breaking meant in relationship to a birth, so I asked her what was going on. She informed me that we could be parents soon—the question was, How soon? I looked at the clock, and it was early. And it was still dark outside.

I was the head of the family, and Mary was looking at me for advice. How would I know? I had never been in this situation before, but my gut said we had better get ready! We lived in El Monte, California, and the doctor and hospital were in Glendale, approximately forty miles away. Under normal circumstances, we may have a couple of hours before the birth of our child; but in Los Angeles, going from El Monte to Glendale during rush hour could take up to three hours. Mary's pains weren't regular or very hard, but I made the decision that we had better get started for the hospital, knowing that it was 5:00 a.m. and there would be traffic. I suggested she call her aunt, who lived in Glendale, to see if we could stop there for breakfast and wait until the critical hour.

We both got ready between contractions and started up the freeway toward Glendale. Each time Mary gasped in pain, my heart jumped into my throat.

Just as we were pulling off the freeway to go to her aunt's house, Mary had a real strong pain and said, "I think we had better go directly to the hospital."

I was really concerned and scared. What if the baby started to come while I was driving? This wasn't good, but how fast should I drive? Should I find a cop? Should we go to her aunt's house or the hospital?

Mary brought me back to earth, saying, "Calm down. We will make it."

I am glad she was more positive than I was. My mind was going fifty miles an hour trying to figure out how fast I needed to drive and whether I should look for a police officer for an escort or I should just stay calm and act as if everything would be okay. We made it to the hospital, and I pulled up in front of the ER. We hurried inside to tell them we were about to have a baby. They told me they were going to take her to the proper floor to examine her and for me to park the car and then go to the admitting station to pick up her registration forms. I did that and then hurried to the third floor. When I arrived on the floor, I asked the ward clerk what room my wife was in, and she told me I was a father. Mary had already given birth to a healthy baby boy!

Oh, yes, the name had been decided back in Red Bluff when Mary and her parents were with me at Lassen Park. We named our son William after my dad. And of course, the last name had to be Woodward. So glad it wasn't Edwards!

It was that close! We arrived at the hospital at 7:25 a.m., and he was born at 7:49 a.m. When the nurse asked me if I wanted to see my new son, of course the answer was yes! The nurse asked me to wait a minute while she got William Walter Woodward ready for me to see. I went to the waiting room, and it wasn't five minutes before she brought out William in a newborn incubator for me to see him. I walked over to look at my son. He was looking up at me with big blue eyes, and I started to weep. For the first time in my life, I had a person who carried my blood. I just couldn't stop crying. The nurse asked if I was all right and if I wanted to hold him. I said yes and yes.

I wanted to publish the news around the world, as all fathers want to do. They had given Mary a spinal block, so she had to lie flat on her back for twenty-four hours, which did not make her happy. She wanted to start taking care of our new son immediately.

A new experience was awaiting—changing diapers and having a mother-in-law living with us. The diapers weren't the kind this sissy generation uses today. They were cloth, with safety pins. When we changed a diaper, we dipped it in the toilet and then put it in a diaper pail to wait for washing. See, you use them over and over again. Shortly after William was born, we moved to La Puente, California, into a real house.

1967–1968

La Puente, California

We celebrated William's first birthday in La Puente. Mary couldn't figure what to make for dinner, so she made spaghetti. This is what you serve a child at the age of one, and he loved it. We put William in his high chair and gave him the plate of spaghetti. It was fun to watch because he didn't use a fork or spoon but both hands. It wasn't long before not only was it in his belly but his hair, his face, and all over his clothes. We just sat there and laughed and laughed. Well, that was just the first course. Mary had made a big first-birthday cake, and he did the same thing with that cake as he had done with the spaghetti—more on the outside than on the inside. It was a great night in the bathtub.

Now, this kid was interesting. I didn't know much, if anything, about raising a child. I tried my best, but I am sure that I could have been much better at the process.

I worked for the insurance company from June of 1966 until the summer of 1968, but I was bored and wanted to do something different. I was hired by an automobile manufacturer as a contract negotiator to negotiate union contracts. Then the plant was going into shutdown for change of models, and I was told to take two weeks off with pay and report around the fifteenth of September.

We headed to San Jose to visit my folks and then join Mary's folks from Red Bluff to take the boat to Lake Powell, Utah, for a week. While we were in San Jose, Dad convinced me to go over and apply at a computer company. I am not sure why I did that; I guess it was to make him happy. I spent almost that whole week interviewing. No offer was made. I informed them that we had vacation plans in Lake Powell with my wife's folks, so I needed to head out. They asked me to call them on the next Friday, and I told them I would.

Off we went to Lake Powell, Utah. When we got to Lake Powell, we loaded the boat and then drove for a good four hours back into Lake Powell to camp. Lake Powell was new and very rough and bare, and some days, we never saw a person as the summer visitors were gone. I learned to water ski and drive a boat and, for the first time, had some quality time with my in-laws. Friday came, and I was supposed to call the computer company. Where was I going to make that phone call? We went over to the marina where we always filled up with gas and asked to use their phone. They laughed because they didn't have a phone. They did tell us that they had a short-wave radio up in Frog's Landing. Off to Frog's Landing we went. When we arrived at Frog's Landing, we found the person with the short-wave radio. He allowed us to get on the radio and contact a person in Salt Lake City who was willing to make a call to the computer company. The call was connected between the short-wave radio, a phone in Salt Lake City, and to the company's location in San Jose. I was offered a position as a system and procedure analyst in the San Jose plant site. I accepted because Mary and I wanted to be closer to our parents. I had no idea what a system and procedure analyst was; but I was told, if I passed a physical on Monday, the job was mine. They would pay to move us from Los Angeles to San Jose.

We quickly headed back to the campsite, packed up, and headed back to the cars. On the way out, I wanted to ski one more time. While I was water skiing, I got tired, but no one in the boat was watching. I kept trying to get their attention and finally just dropped the rope and rested in the water. I watched as the boat disappeared out of sight.

I thought, *Well, they've gotten rid of me forever.*

To my surprise, eventually I saw something heading my way. Sure enough, it was Mary and her parents. They wanted me after all.

We jumped into our Ford Fairlane 500 SS and headed from Lake Powell to La Puente. We knew we would be driving all night, but we weren't worried. We had to get gas in Las Vegas where it was still very hot. We filled the car and then went to put the gas cap back on the car. Well, guess what, I put the gas cap from the car next to us on our car. On the way to Los Angeles, our gas tank was showing empty, so we stopped for more gas. We didn't realize at the time that the gas tank had been sucked in because it was so hot that evening and I had put the wrong gas cap on the car. We had to stop a few more times for gas before we finally got home.

The next morning, I went to the doctor and passed the physical. I began working in San Jose and never said a word to the automobile company. We were on our way to a new adventure in our lives. It is really easy to move when the company comes in and packs all your stuff for you. They also flew us up to San Jose to find housing. They wanted to put us up until we found a place and the furniture arrived. We didn't do that because we wanted to stay with my mom and dad. I am not sure they wanted us, but they wanted to see our two-year-old son, William. We stayed with my folks while Mary and I decided where we might like to live. After Mary chose the area to live, we rented a house. Then we returned to La Puente to get ready for the move to Northern California.

1968–1971

Lencar, Cambrian Park

And so we moved again. This was my nineteenth move, and I was only twenty-eight years of age. I was getting good at moving and even better when the company does all the work.

I had a new job with the computer company and didn't have any idea what it was all about or what I was doing. All I knew was the pay was good, and I was ready to learn. I was assigned a desk in a quad, and my new boss came to me with my first assignment. The job was assigned to me, I believe, because of the work I had done with the insurance company. I was assigned to find out what happened to $1.5 million worth of the company's tooling that was lost. Engineering decided it wanted the tooling back, and when they went to Purchasing to have it returned, Purchasing informed them there must be a mistake because the vendor ID number that Engineering gave them showed it was in the White House of the United States.

Well, how did that tooling get there? I needed to understand the process so I could begin an investigation. I had many meetings with Purchasing, Engineering, and Accounting in smoke-filled conference rooms. It was clear that the right hand didn't know what the left hand was doing. Proper procedures were not being followed. In fact, there were no procedures. Not one of the functional groups understood what the others were doing even though, at times, they had to rely on each other. I soon understood what the problem was—we had three different functional groups in the company who did not communicate with each other. Oh, this new computer age! Each computer system was designed by different people in the programming area. As I talked to each of the functional groups, it was clear they gave requirements to the programming functional group, but they never took the time to cover all the necessary designs to cover the situations with other functional groups on whom they had to rely from time to time. With that said, I started writing a procedure that would cover areas and situations that may arise because of vendor IDs. We didn't ask the White House for that tooling back! We ate the cost because of poor procedures and computer system designs.

Mary enjoyed being a housewife and being with her son all day. By this time, we were ready to have another child. Mary was told that, because she had some female problems, the chances of her having any more children by birth was probably not in the works. Mary and I had always talked about adopting a child to give them the same chance I had received with Mom and Dad. So we started the process, and it wasn't long before we were asked if we would like to adopt a little girl.

We were so excited, and of course, we wanted to adopt her. We named her Amy Woodward, and she was four months old. Now we were the proud parents of one beautiful little girl who joined us on October 23, 1969. Now I will say she wasn't a newborn baby, but I knew the ropes after having dealt with William. At least this time, we didn't have my mother-in-law coming and staying because Mary and I could handle this by ourselves. Amy and William bonded really quickly as brother and sister. William was turning three, and he was going to protect his new sister no matter what. Amy was a very good, beautiful girl whom we both loved very much.

There we were with two children and starting a family that all married people dream about. Amy started really young allowing the cat or dog eat whatever she didn't want to eat. Sound familiar? They enjoyed it, but we knew she was doing that. It was the beginning of her ability to get away with things she didn't want to eat.

A couple of things happened at our rental home in San Jose that are worth telling you about. I was playing for a softball team in San Jose, and I didn't fit in. In fact, during the championship game, one of the players hadn't arrived yet; so they started me. When I came to the plate, I hit a ball way over the head of the left fielder and was sent to home by the third-base coach. I was thrown out as I slid into home. The other player showed up, and I was replaced. I spent more time on the bench than in the field, and the funny thing was both the manager and coach said I was the best hitter on the team. Well, it pissed me off. I picked up my glove, walked to the stands, and told my wife we were leaving. I never played for that team again.

Also, at church, they decided to put on a major program at Easter called "No Greater Love"; and they asked me to be the lead male in the play. I agreed but soon realized I may have made a mistake because this was a very long play with a huge number of lines to remember. I did enjoy doing it after I learned the script. The choir director was an employee of a space division of NASA, so he arranged for the background pictures used at the appropriate times to be pictures from outer space, giving you the view of what God created. This drama was a combination of many actors and actresses, the choir, stagehands, makeup artist, and wardrobe people. It was packed most of the nights, and we did it two years in a row. They wanted to do it a third year, but I told them I did not have the time. Because I wouldn't do it and no one else was willing to take the part, it came to an end. At times, I really felt guilty because I brought a great program to an end.

William had bad tonsils for several years, and they were removed while we lived in San Jose. In fact, when we took him to the hospital to have them taken out, his temperature went above one hundred, so we had to take him home. The hospital staff was sure he was coming down with something. Mary told them that this was what he did and that he would be all right in a few days. We waited a few days, rescheduled, and went back to the hospital to have the tonsils out. This time, success!

It was time to buy a house and start living the good life as a family. The owners of the home we wanted to buy were moving to Oregon, and as they were also friends of my dad, they wanted to put together a deal that would allow us to buy this home. We bought the home with three mortgages on the house although the loan company thought there was only one. To make a long story short, they carried a second, unknown to the mortgage company. Dad threw in his commission, also unknown to the mortgage company, and we got a personal loan from my company's credit union, also unknown to the mortgage company. But we now owned our first home.

A couple of things happened at our home that are worth mentioning. One Christmas, Mary and I bought a Hot Wheels race-car track for William. On Christmas Eve, I had the pleasure of putting it together. In those days, I didn't know the difference between a hammer and a saw. Anyway, I got it put together, or maybe I should say Mary put it together with my limited ability to read the instructions. In the middle of the night, I heard the track working, and I thought it was William playing with it already. I woke Mary up, and the two of us tiptoed out to the family room to watch our son play. Well, we were wrong. Somehow the cat had hit the start button and this car was going around and around the track. Each time it passed, the cat took a swipe at the car. It was really funny seeing this cat watch that car on the track and try to knock it off.

Another incident happened one cold Sunday afternoon. I was a football nut and always watched the games. One particular Sunday afternoon, I decided to have a nice fire in the fireplace while I watched NFL football. I had had a fire in the fireplace a week earlier, and the next day, I was informed I had to clean out the fireplace. I got the metal garbage can and put all the ashes and wood into the can. I put it out in the alley by the house. On this day, I went out to get the can with the fireplace wood. I placed them in the fireplace with more wood, scraped up old paper to start the fire, and lit the fire. Guess what, it wouldn't start up! So smart college grad was going to take care of that. I went to the garage, got a coffee can, and filled it up with gas. The plan was to pour the gasoline onto the wood, light a match, and get the fire going.

I started pouring the gas on the wood, and suddenly the gas caught on fire and ran right up that stream and into the coffee can. You got it—my hands were now on fire! I threw that can, which wasn't a good idea. It hit the couch, but God was with us because William and Amy were not sitting on the couch and it missed them. Now I will say I wasn't quiet because I had just burned my hands really badly. Mary came running, saw the wall was on fire, grabbed a wet towel, and started trying to put the fire out. Since I hadn't closed the patio door, our neighbor heard me screaming and came running. Somehow Mary and Jim got the fire put out, but his wife called the fire department. EMTs took me to ER, and I spent a week with the biggest wrapped hands you have ever seen. Guess what? I never did that again.

One very interesting and exciting thing happened in August of 1971 was when my brother-in-law got married. The bride-to-be asked one of our cousins to be in the wedding. Normally this would be no problem, but my wife's cousin decided she wanted to dye her shoes the same color as the bride's shoes. One small problem: The bride was not buying it, and to be honest, neither did I. Well, that didn't happen. Our cousin's mother was my father-in-law's sister, and she was the type who was not going to be told what she could or could not do. Another problem was that the bride's parents were just like our cousin's mother, and the two parties got quite involved in the matter. As a result, our cousin got kicked out of the wedding—the bride's parents did not want her even coming to the very expensive wedding.

Well, to make things worse, my wife now had three relatives who were very upset; and their statements to the bride's family did not help. I got a call from my father-in-law, the day before they were to arrive, asking how the atmosphere was at the church because my wife and I had gone early to attend the wedding. He asked what his son, the groom, was doing; and I told him he was with the bride's family. This did not go over well, and I knew things were not going to be good when they arrived.

To make things worse, my brother-in-law was not present when his folks arrived. In fact, he was aboard a large sailboat on the Pacific Ocean with his future bride and her family for a major celebration.

This was the beginning of the end of the close relationship between my father-in-law and his son. Up until then, they had been tighter than a first coat of varnish on a pine board. It was clear that my brother-in-law was moving on to a new adventure in his life. He now had a wife, and his dad was not needed any longer as he was in the past. My father-in-law was not ready for this and wanted things to stay close as in the past, and now the balloon had popped.

My brother-in-law and his new wife then travelled up to stay at his dad's house for a few days. I wasn't present, but I later learned it did not go well. His new wife hated snakes, and she required my brother-in-law to go through a magazine and cut out all the snake pictures. He did it, and when my father-in-law found out about it, he just made fun of her. For sure, that did not help the situation between the three of them.

During this time, I decided to hang up my cleats and try coaching baseball. I managed a men's fast-pitch softball team. I chose the players, and we had a nursery company in San Jose sponsor us. In our first season, we went all the way to the regionals. We won the first game but lost the second. It was fun and made me want to continue coaching.

Back on the job, I guessed I impressed someone with that first assignment because the next assignment was to document the product cycle of the company's product. No one had ever done that in the company. As you may remember, I hated English in college. While working for the insurance company, I took many written depositions, and now I was writing documentation for a product cycle. I had a great mind for investigation but a terrible mind for writing. So they had a typing pool of ladies, and I arranged with the manager to use a typing pool of ladies. I would dictate on tape, and they would listen to the tape and transcribe what I said. I found out that, when the tape was sent down, all the ladies wanted to type it up because the manager said they loved my voice. What can I say?

I spent three years at the plant, but then I grew bored and wanted to do something else. The company decided to have a back-to-the-field program. If I were able to convince the proper marketing people that I could become a system engineer or a sales representative, I could change careers. I was able to convince them, and they offered me a position in Des Moines, Iowa. Should I take it? I didn't even know where Iowa was at that time. Would the family be willing to move there? As William and Amy were young, I only had to convince Mary. Mary had been a state park ranger's daughter and had moved many times with her mother, father, and brother. She wanted to do what was best for our family. However, Mary had signed up to go back to college at San Jose State, and William would start Kindergarten in September. If Mary had understood what was going to happen when we moved, I don't believe she would have said yes.

1971–1976

Des Moines, Iowa

Yet another move! I am keeping my average—one move every three years. We left for Des Moines in late October, and we were excited to be there. This was a start of a new career in the marketing field, and it was the first time Mary ever had to drive in snow. The furniture was delivered to our new home just as I was heading off to Cleveland, Ohio, for eleven weeks of marketing training. Mary had to unpack the furniture, drive for the first time in the snow, and learn all about living in Des Moines. I can say she will never let me forget that time.

My brother-in-law and his new wife showed up on their way to England where he was going to be stationed. He had joined the air force and was going to England prior to his assignment in the war. It was nothing like the first experience with them at the wedding. I was able to get to know my new sister-in-law.

For some dumb reason, I also agreed to coach a women's fast-pitch softball team made up of mostly college women who were used to being the starters for their college team or whenever they played. Trouble was there were fifteen on the team and only nine could play at a time. With two pitchers, I was down to thirteen who wanted to play every game. Unfortunately you can only play eight of those thirteen on the field. I learned really fast to stay out of the dugout after I posted the lineup as some of the language was new to me. However, no one quit, and they went on to take second in the regionals. The sponsor of the team and I did not see eye to eye, and I resigned just prior to the regionals. I should have not let the sponsor run over me, threatening me and hurting my pride. Those young ladies had put in so much work, and I believe I let those women down. I will always regret it.

During our time in Iowa, Mary got pregnant with Eric Allen Woodward. This was nearly eight years after our first son, William, was born. Eric was born on August 9, 1974. You may remember this day as being the day Richard Nixon resigned and Gerald Ford was sworn in as president of the United States. The whole time Mary was in labor, I sat watching the proceedings and eating pistachios.

Fortunately my mother-in-law had come to stay with the kids when Mary had the baby. By the third child, I thought I was a pro and could handle anything. As it turned out, Mary had some complications and had to return to the hospital for a few days. I was happy my mother-in-law was there. In those days, you didn't get maternity leave as a father. I had to keep working.

Something happened after this birth. Mary suddenly started to bleed really badly. My mother-in-law was yelling for me to call an ambulance. I called 911 and told them what was going on and went into panic mode. What was I going to do? She couldn't die on me! Then I remembered: A doctor lived two doors down! I headed out the door to get him when a police car came screaming up. No longer had I told him the situation when the ambulance showed up. The paramedics were able to reduce the bleeding, and then we rushed off to the hospital. Thank God my mother-in-law was there to stay with the three kids, and I could go in the ambulance with her. After two days in the hospital, she came home to her family.

Eric was our second son, third child, and really was a good baby. It was clear before long that he had a logical mind, had to understand everything, and could figure out things real fast.

Now the shock of shock. Three months went by, and Mary informed me she was pregnant again. Another one on the way—now this must stop! But I decided to relax and get into the flow of a large family. By now, I was a very experienced expectant dad—I had this down, no problem. It was a nine-month period of being patient and helping with that new little one, who was yet to be a year old. Amy and William were getting old enough to be of help and not a problem.

Mary gave birth to JJ Woodward on August 14, 1975, one year and five days after Eric. It was also the same date we got married but ten years later! I should remind you that, after Mary and I were married, we didn't have much money to spend on our honeymoon in Fort Bragg, California. At that time, I had promised her that, on our tenth anniversary, I would take her anywhere in the world she wanted to go.

She said, "Take me to Iowa Methodist Hospital. At the time, I thought it was very smart of me because I didn't have to spend a lot of money taking her someplace in the world. Now, as I look back at it, maybe it would have been cheaper to take her on that trip. After JJ was born, we decided that our family was complete, and Mary had her tubes tied. Boy, was that close! I didn't need to get fixed. I want you to know that was the last thing on my mind at the time, so don't take that wrong.

In Des Moines, I made sales quota four straight years and four Hundred Percent Clubs. I was named "Salesman of the Year" for which I received a Regional Managers Award. I will never forget my first Hundred Percent Club as it was at the Beverly Hills Hilton Hotel in California. They left no stones untouched to make me happy with lots of activities to do during the day and Hollywood entertainers in the evening. What a life! I had made it!

Because I did so well, they wanted me to team with another salesman to make a great team of salesmen. However, I had a manager who was a jerk. He wanted to find his salesmen unfit for the job when they reached their ninth year. This was my ninth year, and he decided I should not be in the company. So when my evaluation came, he gave me a really bad one in order to start the process of termination. As a team, we had again made the Hundred Percent Club, and we were having none of that. My partner and I decided that we were going to get him. We wrote down all the problems we were having with my boss, and instead of going to his boss, we went all the way to the CEO of the company. The executive vice president of human relations showed up in our branch and later met with me off-site to understand what had happened in our team territory the past year. He told me to go home and wait until he called me. My branch had no idea of the situation until he walked in. My evaluation was changed, and off to San Francisco I went.

Our time in Iowa was one that created some lifelong memories for Mary and me. Des Moines was the start of my marketing career that allowed me to provide well for my family in such a way that would have never happened if I hadn't gone into marketing.

The most important thing I will remember about Des Moines is the birth of the final two members of our family, Eric and JJ. When both of them were born, I had the privilege to be able to be in the delivery room, an experience I will never forget. And it has been a pleasure having those two guys in my life.

Something happened while in Des Moines. Mary's brother and father had a major separation, and I will only say it had to do with my brother-in-law's wife. My father-in-law then became much more interested in his son-in-law, me. It was new to me that someone wanted to do things with me that I like to do and even assist my family moving from Des Moines back to the Bay Area. In fact, my in-laws came out at their expense, helped pack us, load us, and drove the Rent-a-Truck containing all our possessions. It was for sure different from the first time I met him!

1976–1978

Half Moon Bay, California

I was transferred to San Francisco with the same company, where I also made quota for three years and was responsible for marketing to the state of California, its nine universities, and the nineteen state colleges. During this time, I had to become a lobbyist with the State of California. I also marketed to the Presidio of San Francisco and Naval Station Treasure Island. This was my twenty-first move, and I was only thirty-five years of age. Again I was keeping up my moves as this was again a move every two to three years.

I soon found out why I was there. My company sued the state in reference to a bid state. They did not allow us to bid. As a result, the way things were done California was changed. They no longer could write bids to favor one vendor over another. No longer could employees of the state go to outside activities with vendors without reporting it to the controller of the state. With the changes by the state, it became possible for my company to compete.

While that issue was being resolved, I still had to make quota and started trying to find a way to make that quota. In each college, there were college institution groups that were part of the college but were not tied to the college. As a result, they didn't need to go through the normal bidding process as did the actual college. For example, alumni associations are part of the college but not bound by the same rules. I played that to the hilt at all those colleges. For example, I was able to convince the food-vending group that I had a system that would not allow students to give their badges to another student who didn't have a food pass to eat. They installed it, and while I was working on that one, all of the nine universities installed it as well. I made the club those two years I was in San Francisco.

This was also the first time I ever coached football. One night, Mary came home after signing William up for youth football and told me they didn't have a coach for that team. She wanted me to become the head coach of the team so our son could play football. That was a challenge. After meeting with the youth board, I said yes, but I had no idea what I was getting into. I coached youth football for one year, and we had a lot of fun. I learned a lot about football, but our record was 0–10. I also enjoyed very much having the opportunity to coach my son. As any dad would, I made my son the quarterback. I quickly learned that may have not been a very good idea as that put too much pressure on my son.

For some reason, the league had a view of me that I was a good organizer. Peninsula Pop Warner Football League, in the Bay Area, was going to close if someone didn't step up to the plate to lead it. Someone was assigned to contact me about the position. I had no idea who this person was but was asked if I would be willing to attend a meeting to discuss the future of the conference.

Stupid me, I said yes; and before I knew it, I was the commissioner of the Peninsula Pop Warner Football League. The league went from South San Francisco to Gilroy, and now I had to save this program. Well, God gave me great help, and we had a very wonderful season. Except every Saturday and Sunday, I was at games in the Bay Area. For sure, when my sons played, I was at that game. The benefit was that we didn't have to pay to get in. I did this for a while, and before the first year of football was over, my company asked me to take a transfer to Tucson, Arizona.

In our first stay in Half Moon Bay, there was an incident that was a little funny. Mary had come to pick me up from the airport. Since we had to drive down the coast, one evening, we pulled into one of those beach parking locations; I guess to watch the sunset. After a little time, we started making out. Soon we had a visitor. A police officer tapped on the window, and it scared us. We explained we were married with four kids and pointed to our home, which you could see from that spot. We told him we were sorry and headed home. I guess it was an opportunity to be alone without those four rug rats nosing around.

We were much closer to our parents there and were able to see them more. I must say that my in-laws took the time to come down and be with us many times, and my father-in-law and I did a lot of things together.

1977–1980

Tucson, Arizona

I n August of 1978, I was transferred from San Francisco to Tucson, Arizona to become product planning manager. I continued my moves, and this was the twenty-second move! I was thirty-seven years old and still moving just about every two to three years.

During the period of 1978, I was a husband and a dad working hard at my job to support my family. My life was hit with a new trial. Mom and Dad had come to Arizona to spend Thanksgiving and Christmas with us. One night, we went out to dinner; and our oldest son, William, was babysitting the rest. When we returned home, our son informed me that he received a phone call from my "father."

I was confused as my dad was with me, so I said, "Who?"

Will told me he said he was my father. He left a phone number for me to call, so I went to our bedroom and called the number. My birth father answered. Now I was thirty-seven years of age and had never talked to my birth father. I asked him how he found me. He informed me that he was reading the newspaper and saw that an Archie Woodward had passed away.

Since the Woodwards had had custody of me, he was unable to find me. So he called the funeral home and asked to speak to a Woodward. When Ted Woodward, a cousin, answered the phone, my birth father asked him if there was a Juddy Ronald Edwards in the family. Ted told him no but there was a Juddy Edwards Woodward in the family who worked for a computer company and lived in Tucson, Arizona. My birth father then called that computer company in Tucson and asked for my phone number. I am sure he told them he was my father and had lost my number, so the security guard gave it to him. By the way, I reported this to the company on Monday, and they wanted to fire the guard. But since it was Christmas, I asked them not to. They gave him a firm warning never to do that again.

My life had entered a new chapter, but at least I had the support of a loving family. Mr. Edwards and I talked. It was clear to me that all he wanted to do was attack the Woodwards, and I wasn't having any part of that. I informed him he was not my father and that a father is more than a name and not just genes. He had failed both, and I asked him to never call me again. I did have one question for him though. I knew I had a full sister and wondered if she was alive and, if so, where she lived. He told me her present name and the town she lived in, but he had no phone number or address to provide. He informed me he didn't have a relationship with her.

I hung up and went back to my family to answer the questions they had. The strange thing, as I look back, was that Mom and Dad never asked any questions about the situation during their stay. My birth father knew where my birth mother was located, and I received a phone call from her the next evening. It was not good. I could tell she had had too much to drink and she wanted me to call her "Mother" and was very rude. I hung up on her, and because she kept calling, I had my phone number changed and unlisted.

A short time later, I received two letters in the mail. One letter was from my birth father; and the other was from his youngest daughter, who, at that time, was a senior in high school. Both letters, to say the least, did not speak highly of the Woodwards. I wanted to move forward and not answer, but my family had other ideas. With much discussion, I agreed to answer his letter. In that letter, I informed him that he was never to write me again but, if they wanted to exchange Christmas cards, that was okay, as long as they followed the rules. Those rules were not to call or write to me. We could exchange Christmas cards, and that would be our only contact. Through the Christmas cards, we found out that my birth father and his wife had seven other children.

Both my wife and I decided I would try to find my birth sister. So the process started, and after much work, I was able to locate her in Syracuse, New York. I got her phone number and made that phone call. I informed her that I was her brother and, since I was in the area on a business trip, I would like to stop by. She agreed. She asked me to stay with her, and I said no—it was best if I stayed in a hotel.

On Friday evening, I arrived in Syracuse at her home. What I found was interesting as it was clear that she was one of those people who, you would say, were in the lowest income bracket of American families. I was introduced to her partner, who was another female, and four children. After introductions, we left and went to dinner at a restaurant she knew in Syracuse. We had a nice conversation, and I could tell she was so pleased to have me there. I was not sure, at that point, where this relationship was going to go. She filled me in on her life, and it was clear she got the short end of the stick. It was also clear that our birth father's girlfriend didn't want her from the time she returned from Florida and that our birth mother was too busy running across the United States one step ahead of the law. My sister lived a life of casual relationships; and she had four children before getting married—a girl, twin girls, and a son. After she got married, she had four more children. Our dinner ended, and I took her home and told her I would be back on Saturday to spend time with her and her family.

On Saturday, I arrived, and four young children were excited to meet me. We decided to go roller-skating, and then we spent the afternoon and the evening with the family. It was agreed that I would bring my family back to meet them, and I did so a couple of months later. It was a good introduction/reunion, and everyone was polite. I am sure that both her kids and mine were uncertain as to what was really going on and what was next as both of us had young children and the weekend was a strange one. Neither family knew what to expect with the introduction of two very different families. The children learned to get along very fast, and her partner was not there for the weekend. We left, and I stayed in touch with her for a period of time. Then she moved, and we lost touch.

As product manager, I was going to have the opportunity to implement the product cycle I developed in San Jose. I was there on a two-year assignment to learn more about the business. This was a brand-new manufacturing plant for my company, and they moved about six thousand employees from Boulder, Colorado, and San Jose, California. I was one of those people. I had fun as a product-planning manager and learned a lot on that job, but I wanted to do something else. They had just moved in six thousand people, and many more would be coming to Tucson to supply vendors for the new plant.

Many people came who had lots of money to spend on homes, and it became very hard for vendors to react fast enough. We had a problem—many of the people who moved in had too much money. They had sold their homes for much more than the cost of homes in Tucson. Most bought land and started building. We bought a beautiful home but had a problem getting someone to build a wall around our new swimming pool. Before we could put water in our pool, we needed a wall. That gave me a great idea! I went into the adobe-brick wall-building business. Being a salesman, I knew how to estimate costs and where to get product and figure out how to get the walls built. I formed a crew for building walls and handled the clients while the crew did the work. I did that right under the nose of the building department of Tucson, without a building permit or a contractor's license. They were too busy inspecting homes. I did this on the side until we left Tucson.

Again I got a call to coach football since the little guys' coach had quit and they needed a coach. It wasn't my son, but someone had put the buzz in their ear that I had prior coaching experience. But this time, my son wouldn't be on the team. When I took over the team, they hadn't won a game; but because of my last experience, I was much more prepared. We just missed the playoffs, but I had a good taste in my mouth.

I was asked to coach the junior varsity the next year, and this would include my son. I found a good group of football coaches stationed at the air force base in Tucson. I asked them to join me, and this was the start of a very successful football career. Yes, we won the league and lost in the finals of the sections.

Another experience in Tucson I would like to share is when we decided to travel to California and spend some time with Mary's folks. They had a motor home, and it was our plan to borrow it and take a vacation with all the kids to Canada and Yellowstone. Instead, we bought one in California, loaded it with food and supplies, and headed to worlds unknown. I won't bore you with the details, but I must tell you one thing that happened on the trip. There were six of us, which made for interesting sleeping and eating arrangements, but we got around that. When we arrived in Yellowstone after three weeks of traveling, we took the motor home over to Yellowstone Lake to take a hike around the lake. Will was in his early teens and always challenged me to do things. There we were at the lake, and he decided to see who was faster, him or Dad. But there was only one problem—Dad was standing on a slippery log, and when he started running, he fell and cracked his ribs really bad. Off to the Yellowstone hospital we went, and after patching me up, they gave me Demerol. It was great stuff as it took away all my pain, but while driving the motor home, I decided it was time to drive out into the field to see the buffalo up close. That didn't happen because, when I said that, Mary and William took over and I was not allowed to drive again till we arrived in Nampa, Idaho. What killjoys! Those buffalo and I were going to become good friends.

My two years in Tucson came to an end, and it was time to move on. I built a lot of walls and had two very successful seasons as a football coach, and now what? I didn't want to stay in Tucson because I did not like the heat or the job. Some of the things that I will always remember about living in Tucson began with my first visit. After looking at homes, it was clear to me that all the homes looked like cigar boxes situated in the world's largest kitty litter box!

It was time to call in some chips, and I did find several job opportunities. The best-looking job was in Chicago. How was I going to convince my family to move from the warm climate back to the snow country in November? Mary had no problem, but I wasn't sure if the two oldest kids would be happy with the move. However, the kids did enjoy being in the snow. One more time, they were leaving friends and going to another strange place.

With all the above in mind, we headed off to Chicago. There was but one big problem: that motor home. My company would not move it to Chicago, so we decided to drive it. We left Tucson on voting day, November 5, 1980. It was ninety-two degrees in Tucson, and we arrived in Chicago with snow.

1980–1984

Barrington, Illinois

Our motor home was not set up for winter weather; so we had to get it stored and winterized real fast, which we did, but not before the pipes in the shower burst.

We also had a problem with the clothes our kids wore. In Tucson, they wore flip-flops, shorts, and T-shirts which were not acceptable or practical in Chicago. It was winter weather, and since we moved to a "preppy" part of town, the kids needed to wear certain brands to be accepted by the children in our neighborhood. This affected both William and Amy the most. Mary had to get them new clothes in order to be part of the school community.

I want to add a comment at this point in my life. From the time of my marriage until this location, I was a family man who was home in the evening about 95 percent of the time. When we moved to Chicago, my career seemed to move forward in a way I could not even foresee. Travel became my life. Movement to corporate staff was in the cards, and more and more responsibility became part of my life. My only time at home was on Friday night through Monday morning, if not Sunday night. Yes, I traveled so much from then until we moved back to Discovery Bay that I had a million miles accumulated on three different airlines.

From the day that I met Mary, I was aware that she wanted nothing to do with conflict. It even went to the point that she would tell the other person they were right no matter what. I never knew why she was afraid to stand up for her rights or mine when she knew I was right. My mom always was the person who corrected and disciplined, and Dad never did, except for the couple of times I have discussed in the book. Well, I guess the discipline training I learned came from Mom, and up to that point, I was always the one who provided the discipline in our house. As I look back on it now, it was a big mistake in our marriage. Mary always left the discipline for me to deal with, and I just went along with it. However, Will was in high school and trouble. One time, Mary called me while I was in Florida, and she told me I needed to come home immediately as Will's girlfriend's family was very upset. It wasn't anything that Mary couldn't handle, but I still took the next flight home to deal with the situation. This became routine for Mary's attempt to discipline our four kids. To this day, even though they all have moved from home, if I tell them something they don't like, they will call their mother; and she will tell them what they want to hear. I also found out that, during the times I was away, she would tell them not to worry about a situation. She would talk to me and get the problem solved when I got home.

While in Chicago, a few things happened. I got caught up in coaching football again, and my daughter became a cheerleader for our football team. During two of the years I coached, we were 20–0 in league play. We were part of the Lake Zurich Flames football program, where I coached the heavyweight team. Will played freshman football in high school, and Amy took up the flute. Yes, I even attended her concerts, which reminded me of the days when I played in a band.

I'm not sure why, but we bought a twenty-four-foot Sea Ray Cubby Cab I/O boat from a person who stored it next to our motor home. We were entering into a whole new world. Learning to water ski better, pulling a boat behind a motor home, camping, and backing that thing into dock launch with a motor home—these were all new challenges.

Next to us lived a family. The mom took a great liking to Mary, and our two families became good friends. In the summer, when we weren't at a lake camping and water skiing, Mary and I would spend Friday nights with Janet and Jim and head to the Chain O'Lakes where we had the boat moored. We headed off to a different resort on the lake for a great evening. I ate more catfish than ever in my life. Janet was just the opposite of Mary. In fact, one night, after I finished docking the boat, I headed back to the car around midnight. Suddenly I heard a lady singing the "Indian Love Call." I turned around; and sure enough, it was Janet standing by the slip looking up at a full moon with arms raised, singing at the top of her lungs, if you could call it singing. It was not unusual for her and Mary to sing at the top of their lungs at midnight as we crossed the lake to the dock.

We attended Willow Creek Community Church while living in Barrington. The pastor was a very young man, but he was a pleasure to listen to. The church had an active high school program, and every Friday night was teen night. Hundreds of students from all the local high schools attended that evening. Back then, the local high school football games were on Saturday afternoon. I will tell you all the high school girls went to the Friday-night Willow Creek Community Church program, and I always knew where my son William was on Friday night.

Will did a lot of growing up in Barrington and found what girls were all about. I will talk about that in a chapter I have dedicated to my children.

While in Chicago, I again achieved the Hundred Percent Club, making quota. Also I received another Excellence Award for a major project I was asked to head up between my company, a carrier, and a lab. I was then transferred to the headquarters division to market for the telecommunication division. When I again made the quota, I went to the club in Orlando, Florida, where I was informed that I was being named president of the telecommunication division club and would be honored at the club. With it came an invitation to their Golden Circle. This honor was for the "best of the best" marketing people in the company. Mary and I had the wonderful opportunity to attend the Golden Circle in Kauai, Hawaii, and enjoyed it very much. The entertainment was Sammy Davis Jr., Dick Clark of *American Bandstand*, a sock hop with an ice-cream social, and an evening enjoying the piano majesty of Roger Williams. The last evening at the club, we had the pleasure of listening to a concert by the one of the Rat Pack, Sammy Davis Jr.

We also used this opportunity to have a major vacation after the Golden Circle with our four children. We met three of them in Honolulu. I used my air miles and sent three on one airline and William on another. William's plane was delayed. We found out that it had to go back to Los Angeles to refuel before making it across the Pacific. I stayed in Honolulu while Mary and the three went on ahead to Maui. William and I stayed in a hotel that night and joined them in the morning for a wonderful trip.

Back in Chicago, my company decided to get into the telephone business by building a digital switch. As I was in the telecommunication division, I was told that I was going to have the lead on the project reporting to our company president. My company understood that it could never market the product as this was a cut-throat business. I was commissioned to find a vendor who would like to market our product. After giving it some thought, I determined the best vendors were the independent telephone companies, and the company I chose was located in Chicago.

The president of my company flew in, and we met with the CEO of the independent telephone company. In case you ever get that opportunity, let me tell you something: Every major company has a profile on its officers, and you should request one so your executive will have a chance to understand whom they are meeting, including information from college, family, and career experiences. Our president was flying into Chicago, so I left the profile of the CEO at his hotel room the night before so he would have an opportunity to read it before the meeting.

When the two of us went to the telephone company, we found a group of executives in the room ready to hear our offer to their company. They listened, asked lots of questions, and told us yes and they would like to be sole vendor of our digital switch. An executive vice president was assigned to work with me to bring a happy conclusion for both companies.

The switch was being built in Fort Lauderdale, Florida, and I was traveling almost every week between Chicago and Fort Lauderdale. This executive vice president and I traveled to Florida to review the progress of the switch. Some corporate officers of my company, however, didn't know if they wanted to build a digital switch or not. They thought it would be better to buy a company that already had one.

There were some conflicts between executives on the corporate management committee. As a result, I had to go to the telephone company a few times to inform them we had decided not to do the digital switch. Later I went back to tell them we had decided to go ahead and build it with them. Each time I made that call on my friend, the executive vice president, he accepted my announcement with grace.

About two weeks later, our division president called me and had some very bad news. The telephone company's management committee had met, and they decided they were going to purchase a digital switch company instead of making one. Under no circumstance was I to give any indication that we were about to purchase a digital switch company. With that said, I told him I needed to leave Chicago; my career there was over. I told him I needed him to do something for me—I wanted to be moved. He asked me where I would like to go. I didn't hesitate and said San Francisco. He had no problem with that. I did my part, and he did his part. The Woodward family was heading west once again!

William, who was now a senior, and Amy, a sophomore, wanted to return to Half Moon Bay. On our house-hunting trip, after searching the entire Bay Area, we finally found a home in Half Moon Bay. We had already sent William to start school and to join his old friends from fourth and fifth grade.

We had sold the motor home and still had the boat, but my company would not move that boat. We decided to pull the boat across the United States with our GMC van after our furniture was packed and shipped. We arranged with my in-laws to pick up the kids (less William, who was already there for football) at the Sacramento Airport and keep them in Red Bluff until we arrived.

Mary and I, with two dogs, headed to California pulling the twenty-four-foot boat. The first problem was I had never towed anything that far, and I had to get used to driving slower and paying attention to road grooves. We left Illinois and got a far as Wyoming and had another problem. The brakes on the boat trailer went out. I drove carefully until the next town and hoped we could get them fixed. Driving with just the van brakes took some skill going very slowly down hills; but we made it, got them fixed, and again headed west. The next problem was that California would not allow some of the houseplants that Mary wanted to bring to our new home. Mary decided to put those plants in the boat until it was full of plants.

Now about the plants. We did some research; and as we were going to leave the boat up at the Walnut Ranch in Red Bluff and our children were there, we found that, if we went up 395 to Susanville and crossed the California border at that point, there was no California checkpoint. So off we went to satisfy Mary and her plants.

The road between Susanville and Red Bluff was not for the faint of heart. There were very steep grades, and it was a windy two-lane road all the way up and down going over Mt. Lassen. Just before we left Susanville, I filled up with gas. The problem was that it was the only gas station and the last stop before we headed up. Leaving that gas station was just the start. As soon as we hit the main street, there was a very steep grade which I took at about five miles an hour for the first five miles before I hit some level ground to build up speed. When we started, I didn't believe we were going to make it. In fact, there were times I believe I was going to blow that GMC engine or transmission, all to bring a few illegal plants into California. The good Lord was all for Mary, and we made it up the hill and then down the hill. Miles and miles of brake use, around winding narrow roads we traveled. To say the least, I was a nervous wreck when we finally arrived in Red Bluff all in one piece. I guess keeping the wife happy was the most important part, and I achieved that one more time. After a couple of days of rest, we loaded the three kids into the van and headed to our new home in Half Moon Bay.

1984–1993

Moss Beach, California

After that exciting trip to California, which took five years off my life, we were back in California for my fifth time. We had put an offer on a home, and before closing, the inspection reports did not look good. In fact, it was very bad. The inspector said the house would have to be jacked up with a new foundation under it to correct the problem. Well, we decided not to buy the house. Our furniture was on its way, but we had no home. We arranged with the union who owned the home for us to move in until we found something else. Mary then found a piece of property she wanted to buy and build a home.

My first thought was "You're crazy!"

We were going to build a house! We knew nothing about building, but she reminded me we added on to our home in Iowa. I laughed because building a house is a lot different from adding onto a house. I lost that argument, and the picture above shows the home we built. So with faith, we bought the land. I had a nephew living in Idaho who was a contractor, and we wondered if he might consider the job of building our house. It was mid-October, and we agreed that he would start the job in January but had to be finished no later than April because we had a six-month lease on our Half Moon Bay house. He agreed since there's not too much building in Idaho during the winter. He jumped at the chance. The good news was that the building plans were already drawn up and permits approved by the county. You know Mary; she didn't like the plans the way they were and wanted to revise them completely.

I became the contractor as I owned the property; and oh, by the way, we had to revise the heat calculations, window specs, and truss specs, in addition to having the foundation approved by a geologist, in order to get the building permit approved. We also had to get subcontractors and materials bids and purchase all the cabinets, appliances, fixtures, etc. This all had to be done before April with a certification of completion on April 1. We had a short-term lease on the home we were living in with an understanding that, if the union got an offer and sold the house, we would be out in sixty days. Plus I needed to get our additional furniture out of storage, or my company would not be happy.

Oh, by the way, I had a real job with the responsibility of Northern California, Oregon, Washington, Wyoming, and Alaska for my company. I had four kids in school, three additional guys living in our home, and furniture in storage. One child was a senior playing varsity football; another was a sophomore getting situated with old friends, one in fifth grade, and another in fourth grade. In

January, we would have a home with two children and seven adults to care for with cooking and cleaning, all while making sure the house got built the way Mary wanted. Mary made breakfast, lunch, and dinner for at least eight people if I wasn't around.

During the construction, if I went to the county to schedule inspections or make changes to plans, there was a fifty-fifty chance they would be approved. We learned really quickly, if we wanted something done at the site that affected the building, we would send Mary. This good-looking blonde could get those guys at the county to approve anything. This sure helped in meeting our building deadline. She got it done.

I had difficulty working on the house while trying to do my real job that I was getting paid to do. Two weeks of every month were spent on the project, and the other two were on the job with my company. Don't tell them. Plus I was watching football games and any other activities the children were involved in on the weekends. I had to fly back east for staff meetings at least once a month. But we got the house completed, and we did move in the first of April. We met another deadline! Did I age? No, it was fun.

As the house was being built, I got a phone call from the emergency room of a hospital in San Jose. It was about my mom. She was a very ill because she had had a heart attack. I headed to San Jose with Mary and arrived to find Dad sitting in ICU with Mom. I could see that Dad was very worried and really tired. Around midnight, after some discussion with the ICU nurse, I asked Mary to take Dad home. He didn't want to go, but he only lived five minutes away. I assured him that, if she got worse, I would call Mary right away. He and Mary left, and I looked at the nurse and asked how bad was it. My mom was a serious diabetic and ate everything she so desired. So for some time, we knew it was only a matter of time.

The ICU nurse did not have good words. She told me that, when they inserted the trach to make breathing easier, they damaged her vocal cords and she couldn't talk. They were not sure if she ever would talk. That gave me a bad feeling, and the nurse also told me the next forty-eight hours would tell the story.

As it was after midnight and Mom wasn't going to die, I decided I would wait to contact Bob and Shirley the next morning. I spent the night in Mom's room watching the machines, but I had no idea what they were for. The ICU nurse came in every thirty minutes to assure everything was going okay.

In the morning, I called my brother, Bob, and told him what had happened. I let him know that, if he wanted to see Mom alive, he'd better come quick. He informed me that they would leave that day. I then called my sister Shirley and told her the same. She told me she would fly out from Binghamton, New York. I told her she could stay at Dad's and that someone would pick her up at the airport when she arrived.

Mary and Dad showed up and then the doctor. Dad asked the doctor if he could speak with him in the hallway. The two went out and had some kind of discussion and then returned. Dad asked to see me, so when we went out into the hallway, Dad let me know that he told the doctor to take orders only from me.

Bob and Belle showed up the next day, and so did Shirley. As I hadn't had any sleep, I decided to head home even though I knew Mom could die while I was sleeping. The next morning, when I arrived at the hospital, Mary, Bob, Belle, Shirley, and Dad were in the room. As soon as I entered the room, they all told me the doctor wanted to talk to me. I went out to the nurse's station and asked to talk to the doctor. They called his office, and he told me that Mom wasn't going to make it but she could have a couple of more months if they put in a pacemaker to assist her heart. When we talked about her voice, he didn't think she would be able to talk. Boy, did Mother love to talk! And she would only have a few months. With that, I said no. I didn't want to put Dad through any more pain, especially if she wouldn't be able to talk. I never thought I would be in that position. I walked into the room, and everyone asked what the doctor wanted. I told them and my decision, and everyone looked at me and said I made the correct one, except Dad didn't say anything. Bob, Belle, and Shirley spent the whole day with Mom; and Shirley stayed through the evening. Shirley told us Mother wrote on a whiteboard to communicate. To this day, I believe that Mom was going to live until she saw her daughter. After that, life was at an end.

It wasn't long before you could tell Mom was going to pass, and Shirley took my hand. She told me to look at Mom's feet, which were turning purple.

I said, "I know. It's not long now."

It was dinnertime, so I suggested that they go and eat and that Mary and I would stay with her. Dad did not want to go; so Shirley, Bob, and Belle left to go eat.

Dad stayed by her bed holding her hand. Mary sat in a chair at the end of the bed while I was on the other side watching the heart monitor. It wasn't long before it went flat. The alarm went off, and I told Dad she had died. He looked at me and said she was still breathing. I said no. It was the oxygen tube attached to her throat, and it was causing her chest to go up and down.

One of the emergency-room doctors showed up and pronounced that she had passed away. I knew there were people in the waiting room from church because I would go out and talk to them from time to time. I went to the waiting room and informed them of her passing. We all prayed, and they left.

We waited until Dad wanted to leave her. He kissed her on the cheek, and I gave her a kiss on the forehead. We then left to go find Bob, Belle, and Shirley. We told them what happened and made sure Dad was okay to stay with them. We knew he would be in good hands, so Mary and I headed home to tell our kids Grandma had passed away.

The whole family planned the service, and Dad insisted that Mary sing at the funeral. We had a celebration of her life at the church Dad and Mom attended. After the service, I really broke down. My son Eric came to me and put his arms around me to comfort me. I was so thankful for that, and he held me close. As I write this, tears come to my eyes. I never felt closer to my son, and I knew I loved him so much.

Life changed. The woman who raised me was no longer around; but I knew without any question, if there was a heaven, Mom was there looking down on us. A strong disciple of God had just passed away. For some time, when I was walking into Dad's home, I would look at the chair Mom always sat in, expecting to see her there. We took care of the legal issues with Mom's death, and because Shirley was going to stay for a couple of weeks, I knew Dad would be okay.

> Death leaves a heartache no one can heal;
> love leaves a memory no one can steal. (Author unknown)

I would be remiss if I didn't say a couple of things which have always been a serious part of my life. I always knew that, out of us three children, I was very much third on her list. I know Mom said things to me that she never told the other two. Things like "Sorry we ever took you" and "I wish we could send you back." But that was only when she was mad at me. Of course, everyone knows a person's true feelings when they say things out of anger.

Also, all my life until I was about twenty-five years of age, I believed that Mom and Dad were always married; but when it was about time for their fiftieth wedding anniversary, I started talking about it. At dinner one night with Mary, Mom and Dad informed me that Mom had been married before and that Dad had adopted Bob and Shirley. It was a shock! Why did they keep that from me? But a bigger problem was that Mary already knew it and never told me.

And at some point in our marriage, Mom said to Mary, "If you want to divorce him, it is okay with me."

I never heard about this until after her death. Mary was very good at informing me of these types of issues long after the fact. The longer I lived, the clearer it became to me that Dad wanted me and forced the issue since Bob and Shirley were her children and not Dad's.

This also started me questioning the premise that I had always believed: God first, wife or husband second, children third, and then everything else. I started questioning in my mind if my wife loved me as God dictates.

Another situation that happened at this time was when my seventeen-year-old daughter, Amy, a senior in high school, got pregnant. When my wife informed me, it was clear that I was to handle the situation. This should have been a situation where mother, father, and daughter decided what was the best thing to do, both at the present and for the long term. But Mary wanted nothing to do with it. Her position was, whatever my daughter and I decided, she would support. My daughter and I came to an agreement that she could have the baby and keep it, give the baby up for adoption, or have an abortion. She had three weeks to decide because, after that, option three would be gone.

My daughter decided to have the abortion. My wife joined us at the abortion center but did not agree or disagree with my daughter's decision. She just didn't want anyone to think badly of her for what her daughter chose to do. After the abortion, my daughter and I drove home. I made it very clear that, if this ever happened again and if she was underage, she was going to have the child. I did not support abortions. It was one of the hardest things I ever had to do because I fully understood what it felt like to be unwanted.

My job required I travel to the East Coast about once a month for a staff meeting. One afternoon, while living there, just south of San Francisco, I received a phone call from a person who said she was a nurse at a hospice. She told me my birth father was dying of lung cancer and that he wanted to see me before he died. I told her I didn't think I wanted to meet him but I would discuss it with my wife and get back to her. She gave me her phone number. The family talked me into going, but I would go only if Mary went with me. She agreed. We decided that we would fly from San Francisco to New York City, go see my birth father, and then fly from New York to Hawaii for a vacation. It was also going to be our anniversary, so as my dad would say, we were going to "kill two birds with one stone." We made plans and, in the process, were informed that my cousin Ted Woodward—yes, the one who told my birth father where I was in 1978—was in the hospital in the same town with a heart condition. The agreement was that we would meet with my birth father and his wife but no one else in the family.

When we arrived in town, we went to see my cousin in the hospital and then moved on to the hospice to see my birth father. As we entered the room, we saw they had violated the agreement. His wife, my half brother and his wife, and my youngest half sister and her husband were all there. I wanted to leave, but Mary wouldn't let me. My birth father never said hi to me.

His first words I remember well were "You sure have a good eye for women!"

We had a conversation for about two hours, and then we left for Hawaii. It was sad. He had smoked for years. He tried to get treatment for his situation, and you could tell he was at peace with death. Information I have received through my investigation revealed why he may have wanted to die.

A few months later, I was in Raleigh, North Carolina, at a staff meeting. The company management asked if I would be willing to make a call on executives in both Pittsburgh and New York City the following week. I had plans for the weekend back home. But the person responsible for covering that territory had lost his son in a terrible accident that week, so I agreed to do it. I flew back to San Francisco Friday afternoon and then back to Pittsburgh on Sunday evening. The good news was that the first visit was on Monday and the second visit was on Wednesday, which left me Tuesday to rest up from the short weekend. Saturday morning, I received a phone call from my half brother and his mother informing me that my birth father had died and they would appreciate it if I would attend the funeral service. I asked when the service would be, and they told me it was on Tuesday. Interesting—a meeting on Monday and a meeting on Wednesday back East but nothing on Tuesday. I told them I would discuss it with the family and then get back to them. I hung up; and as we were discussing the situation, I received another phone call from my sister Shirley that my cousin Ted Woodward—yes, the same person who told my birth father where I was and whom I visited prior to visiting my birth father on his death bed—had passed away. I asked when that funeral would be, and Shirley said it was the next Tuesday afternoon.

The family insisted that we attend, but Mary could not attend on such short notice. I was on my own this time. On Sunday afternoon, I headed east to Pittsburgh to make that company meeting and then spent most of the day with the executives. Afterward I caught a plane to Binghamton, New York, where I met my sister Shirley; and then we went to the funeral home to pay our respects to my cousin's family. I knew everyone there, and they were all surprised but very glad to see me. After that, I headed to the other funeral home knowing that, for the first time in my life, I was going to meet many people I had never met, an uncomfortable situation.

As I started walking into the funeral home, I heard voices saying, "Here he comes!"

I was in my corporate blues. As I entered, people started talking to me, and I had no idea what they were saying. In fact, the attention turned from the person in the casket to me, and I became the center of attention. I just kept my head and flowed with the situation.

After a while, it was time to go, and the family asked me to join them for dinner. It was after nine o'clock, and as I hadn't eaten, I agreed. It was clear I had overdressed for the occasion, so I left my jacket and tie in the car as we went to eat.

The next morning, I had breakfast, but I was not in a hurry to head for the funeral home. I called a cousin, Clara, and her husband, Buzz, and asked if I could visit them until the time of the first funeral. At about fifteen minutes before the funeral, I told them I'd see them the afternoon and headed for the funeral home. I arrived and was greeted by one of the funeral personnel as I pulled in. He asked me my name and told me my car was to be directly behind the hearse. I said no way, but he informed me that the family had already instructed the order. As time was short, I told him I would take care of it later and headed into the funeral home. Yes, I was in my corporate blues; and yes, I was very much overdressed. I took a seat in the very back of the funeral home and was sitting there with a crowd of about 150 people when my half brother, full sister, and my birth father's wife got up and headed my way. They asked me to come forward and sit with the rest of the family. I didn't want to but also didn't want to cause a scene. I felt like every eye in that place was looking at me. I agreed and followed them to the front where my birth father's children were all sitting in the front row, without spouses, according to age. They asked me to sit in the first seat with his wife next to me, and after that, it was my full sister on down to my youngest half sister. The funeral director came forward and opened the casket, and a minister came from a side door and addressed the family. He presided over the service, and it was clear to me that this family did not go to church and that he didn't know my birth father. I had no feeling whatsoever as the rest of the family shed their tears.

At the conclusion of the service, the funeral director came forward and looked at all the attendees and informed them that they were invited to pass the casket and pay their respects to my birth father. After he said that, he called out his wife's name, and she was to stand next to the casket.

Then he said, "Mr. Juddy Woodward."

Talk about surprises! And what was I to do? This was one of those situations you are not taught how to handle. I was shocked but got up and moved next to the wife, and we thanked the people who attended my birth father's funeral. This was planned without my knowledge, and a funeral was not the time to cause a scene.

After they all left and just the family was present, I quietly went outside alone and found my rental car sitting right behind the hearse. I turned around and saw the rest of the family coming. I asked if I could have a word with his wife and my half brother. I informed them I was not the head of this family and either they move my car to the back of the family cars or I would get in my car right now and leave. When I got to my car, a few nieces I had never known wanted to ride with their Uncle Juddy. To this day, I have no idea who they were as they were very young.

After the cemetery service and a short visit with my birth father's relatives, I asked to see my half brother. I apologized for what had happened at the funeral. I told him I was not the head of that family and was so sorry he was cut out of his rightful place in the family. I left and went to the other funeral, my cousin's, hoping I had no more surprises.

When I returned home to my family, I took the time to reflect on the past three days. It was clear to me that each one of my birth father's family members loved him very much. He was their dad, and the tears were real. Discussion with my wife left me with a mixed mindset. Should I just move down the road of life that I had lived over the past forty-six years, or should I extend a hand of friendship to a family I did not know but was my blood. My wife and I decided to extend that hand. After much thought, we decided that we would invite my birth father's wife to California to spend some time with our family. We extended the invitation, and since we understood the economic situation of that family as I had witnessed, we also told her the trip was on our family. There was a problem. She had never flown and was afraid to fly by herself. So the invitation was extended to one of her daughters and her husband to join his wife. The time spent together was very interesting. Everybody handled the situation as if we were walking on eggshells. The daughter asked me if we were going to be brother and sister. I avoided the question and really never gave an answer. Also my half sister asked if she could borrow money, and it wasn't a small amount. Without wanting to cause a scene, we agreed with understanding that we were going to be paid back. I had to get my half brother involved in order to receive our money. The funny thing is that, that sister, out of the five other half sisters, became my best friend in the family. She informed me more than once that she moved to Texas to get away from the rest of her family as there were too many issues. Prior to her death, we always talked three or four times a year on the phone.

When they left, we felt it was a good visit. But they lived in New York; I lived in California. It would be better if I just moved forward with the life I had lived for the past forty-six years. Plus I didn't want to confuse my younger children with the situation of my life.

I should say, at that time Mary was in college at San Francisco State and majoring in consumer and family services, I had one child in elementary school, one child in junior high, one child in high school, and one child in junior college; and my wife going to college full-time. During this time, I was still doing my job with my company and traveling extensively.

Soon after we completed building our house, we decided we needed to do something with our boat, which we kept in Red Bluff three hours away. What should we do? Mary's parents owned a walnut orchard they called "the Cracked Nut." We also discovered that

Mary had a cousin who lived in Clear Lake, California, about two hours away. We decided to get a boat slip at the place, buy a motor home, and park it at a park with a boat dock and spend the weekends at the lake. Luckily we found a spot right next to the lake and built a slip and a deck so we could go up each weekend to enjoy the lake as a family. We drove two hours up there on Friday night or Saturday morning and then two hours back on Sunday night.

My job did not allow me to coach football, so I agreed to be regional director of Pop Warner Football for the same territory I was responsible with my company. How stupid could I be? Another responsibility? Was I neglecting my family? It meant I would sit on the board of directors of Pop Warner Football and have to attend two board meetings a year and have two regional meetings with those football conferences. In addition, I had to attend the football scholar/athlete banquet that Pop Warner had for all national football players and cheerleaders who had outstanding grades. The good news was that the banquet was the same time as one of the annual meetings for the Pop Warner Corporation. One year at that football scholar/athlete banquet, without my knowledge, the president of Pop Warner came to me ask me to speak to the group for about thirty minutes. Now this was a very large group of kids and parents from all over the United States, pro football players, and owners of NFL teams. What was I going to talk about? I was a filler because the CEO was late showing up for the banquet. Well, I did it. I don't remember what I said, but I sure was glad when the CEO showed up and I only had to talk for fifteen minutes. I will say that, during my time as regional director and member of the corporate board of directors, Joe Robby, owner of the Miami Dolphins, was CEO. Upon Joe's death from cancer, I resigned my positions on the board and as regional director.

I got a call that my company had a job they wanted me to do. The CEOs of three major companies had gotten together for breakfast. Sometime during that breakfast, they decided to see if the three companies could work together, and they had a big bid that was coming out that fit each business to a T. The CEOs were from a communication company, a digital telecom switch, and a software company to make it all work together. They brought up my name as the person to head up the endeavor. I would report to two of the CEOs, and I would have a direct line to each company's president to keep them informed on the status of our goal in order to win the bid. They told me I would no longer have the northern territory for my company. What did I do wrong? I needed this like I needed another hole in my head. As a good solider, I took the job, not sure I even had a choice. I assumed I was chosen because of the work I had done in Chicago building a digital telecom switch as well as my experience in the outside vendor market for my company.

It took a total of six months, Monday through Thursday in Los Angeles. Each Thursday night, I took the red-eye from LAX to Washington Dulles to have a meeting with the executives of each company to review the progress. After the meeting, I would grab a plane back to San Francisco so I could watch my boys play football or spend some time at the lake with my family prior to flying back to Los Angeles on Monday morning.

In the middle of this project was the World Series. I left work a little early to make sure I saw the first game. I was changing clothes in my hotel room and getting ready to head downstairs to a private party with a large screen, and before I left my room, the TV broadcast I was watching was interrupted. I sat in my room watching the news. The announcers were shaken and said that San Francisco and the surrounding area had just had a major earthquake. Of course, at that time, they didn't know how bad it was. As the coverage continued, I became very worried about the safety of my family. I made a phone call to my home and was lucky Mary answered, and she was scared. She said the earthquake just rolled through the house. Eric and JJ were at football practice, so I had no idea how they were. Amy was due home from work anytime. The good news was that my son William was in college in San Diego.

I didn't hesitate; I headed home! For sure, planes were not going to be flying into Oakland or San Francisco, so I flew into an airport south of the Bay Area. I then took a rental car north to be with my family. What route should I take? It was clear all the bay bridges were closed, so going up I-5 was not a good option. I wasn't sure about Highway 101. I decided to just head north and play it by ear. I got lucky and had no problem getting home. I found everyone okay. I arrived about two in the morning, but I didn't care. This was on October 17, 1989. My family was shaken but safe. And there was no damage to our house.

The problems the earthquake caused are history, and you can read about it in history books. The special project I was to head up still had to be finished. I got back to Los Angeles and wrapped up the job and received an Excellence Award with a nice check, the third one in my career.

Then the dream job came. I was asked to have the revenue responsibility for my company in Southern California, Arizona, and Hawaii. I also was asked to cover Area 10; and that was not good since it included Texas, Louisiana, and New Mexico. It was summertime, and that area was really hot and humid. But as a good employee, I agreed. The good news was I had it for only about three months before they promoted a person to take it over. Life was great!

While living in Moss Beach, we celebrated one of the major events in life: our twenty-fifth wedding anniversary. Mary wanted to go to Scotland to see the Weaver Castle, which was in her family. We flew into Manchester, England, and for the first time, I had the opportunity to drive an English stick-shift auto on the wrong side of the road. After we put the luggage into the boot, I entered the car on the wrong side and found I was going to drive the car from the right and use my left hand to shift. I couldn't find reverse for the longest time. I also had to drive with my left foot on the gas pedal and my right foot on the brake. Then, as we were leaving the airport parking lot, I tried to exit the entrance and just about ran over those spikes. Ouch, that would have hurt!

We headed off to the castle. But it was a long drive, and we had jet lag. We needed to find a place to stay prior to arriving at the castle. We found a hotel and told them we were celebrating our twenty-fifth anniversary, so they gave us the honeymoon suite! That was an interesting room, especially the tub, the color, size, and all the jets. What a night we had!

We went to dinner, and I did something stupid. I ordered a perfect Rob Roy over with a twist. Off went the waiter to get my drink.

After a while, he came back and asked what was in that drink. I told him, and a little while later, he came back with my drink. It was in a very tall glass and filled to the top.

I looked at him and said, "What is this?"

"Your drink," he said.

"No, that is not my drink! What did you put in it?"

He told me; and believe me, if I had drunk that, I still would be drunk or dead. I asked him to take me to the bar, where I asked the bartender if he had ever made a Rob Roy. His answer was no.

I said, "If you don't mind, let me make it, and you watch."

He agreed, so I made the drink while Scottish people at the bar watched. Afterward he took a sip and loved it! He then passed the drink around so those sitting at the bar could try, and they all loved it. I made another and went back to eat.

The next morning, off we went to the castle. The last stage of the drive was a one-lane road, and I prayed that I didn't meet any vehicles until I arrived. When we arrived, we were welcomed to the castle. Mary signed the family book, and our luggage was taken to the Rose Room, which is reserved only for Rose family members. This was a very large room with no heat except the fireplace. You have to remember this castle was built in the tenth century and with very thick stone walls. Updating it with heat, electricity, and plumbing was a real challenge. Our first experience was the bathroom because the shower, toilet, and sink were all together. When you took a shower, you could take it while sitting on the toilet!

We spent four days at the castle. On the day of our anniversary, they had prepared a room in the castle for Mary and me to have our anniversary dinner in private. We didn't want that because we wanted to share this moment with the rest of the people lodged in the castle. There were around fifteen people staying there, and we joined them instead. After dinner, we all moved to another room where they brought us all tea, and in came a very large cake. The icing was marzipan with silver embellishments, and the cake was almost like fruitcake, very heavy. This was an experience we all enjoyed: this heavy cake with a nice cup of tea.

During our stay, we visited the Loch Ness Monster location and went to a few woolen mills to find some fabric for the Weaver tartan. We also bought a Weaver crest. Mary, queen of Scots, stayed at the castle at least one time and reigned over Scotland from 1542 until 1567.

Back in those days, if you wanted to enter the castle, there was no front door like today. There was a rope, and you pulled on it. A bell would clang, and soon a person would look down. If you were someone they wanted to let in, they dropped a rope ladder, and you climbed up. That was a security alarm system of the day.

We headed back to Edinburgh, Scotland, to see the Tattoo Festival. This year, at the festival, the United States Marine Band was representing the United States. This festival is for the month of August and takes place in the courtyard of the Edinburgh Castle. Many countries send the bagpipe and fife corps for all to see and hear. It was really great, and if you ever get the chance, head to Edinburgh in August and enjoy this great festival. I have been to Edinburgh a few times, and for your young people, I understand that one of the major places in the world to spend New Year's Eve is Edinburgh.

We then traveled on down to London to spend a few days. As this was our first trip there, we were in awe of all the things to see in London. We went to a Broadway show called *Cats* in Piccadilly Square and watched the changing of the guard at Queen Elizabeth's castle. We visited Westminster Abbey, learned the subway system, and, most of all, got our real first experience of currency exchange. At that time, £1.00 equaled $1.90.

We had a great time, but time to go back home. When we got home, we had a big surprise! Amy had arranged a twenty-fifth-anniversary surprise party for us. All our friends and relatives were present, and it was so much fun. This was 1990. The year 1991 turned out to be a very interesting year. William was going to graduate from college in May and was also engaged and planning to get married the following May.

We reserved the executive suite of a San Diego hotel for his graduation party, and it was a big success. I do remember that we brought Dad with us. As he watched this whole process, he took me aside and apologized for not attending my college graduation. If he had known it was such a big deal, he would have been there. Now you have to understand Dad only had an eighth-grade education and never knew what it was like to attend any graduation. In fact, he didn't attend Bob's when he graduated from college.

Later that year, Amy met a young man she wanted to spend the rest of her life with. I will discuss this further in the family chapter, so be sure that you read that interesting chapter. At the wedding, we had dinner at the South Shore Yacht Club in Lake Tahoe, California, in a private room. Then off we went to the gambling casino. Amy and her husband have been married for twenty-six years and have two boys—Eddie, age twenty-five, and William, 22.

Then came another wedding. A young lady, Lisa Ann Smith, attended college with William and was able to hog-tie him. Her daddy, Mont, was a doctor. Well, that wedding was held in a beautiful small church on Coronado Island. The reception was held at the Hotel del Coronado in the grand ballroom. I was glad I wasn't paying for that wedding. In fact, to this day, when I see Lisa's dad, he tells me he is still paying for the wedding.

Then in March of 1992, my world crashed. As you remember back when I was told by Pauline Woodward that they were going to move to California, I said it hit me that I was a boy without a family and I needed to control my life and have financial security. For the first time in my married life, I felt I had just lost both.

My company announced they were going cut 110,000 employees in the United States. I was a corporate employee at the age of fifty-two with twenty-eight years of service, and they placed me on the surplus list. I had until August of that year to find another job within my company. They eliminated certain groups, including the group I happened to be in. The downsizing was headed by human resources, and they targeted people who had been in the company a long time and who had high salaries. They reasoned that they could hire younger people at a much lower cost. Now I was in shock. The computer company plan was to give me two weeks' pay for every year of service, and if I was old enough to retire and get my pension, I could retire with benefits.

The requirement to retire was either fifty-five years of age or thirty years of service. Well, my age was fifty-two, not fifty-five; and twenty-eight years of service was not thirty. My world came crashing down around me. I was no longer in control and was about to lose financial security. I had one child in college and one in high school and couldn't believe this was happening. A lot of groups on the East Coast and Midwest in the marketing division wanted me, but a freeze had been put on the West Coast in marketing. Mary and I were not going to move from the West Coast then because all of our kids were in California.

I was able to find a position in the San Jose plant site of a company to be in charge of worldwide business shows for their products. The San Jose plant was over two hours away from our home in Moss Beach. So out I went from corporate to a manufacturing division and moved to the new job in San Jose, the same place I started so many years ago. I was also able to get a moving and living expense. This meant the new company would buy our home and pay the closing costs on both homes plus our moving expenses. We had had this privilege on all our moves since that first move from Los Angeles to San Jose in 1968.

In June, I started with the new division, and it was not good. I wasn't used to being inside all day, and it felt like the walls were crashing in on me each day. After about a month, I knew this was not going to work.

In August of 1992, I crashed. I had a total nervous breakdown to the point that I tried to commit suicide. I guess God's hand was involved. After I took the pills, for some reason, I got a call from my doctor; and I told him I was going to die and hung up. He knew that Mary was teaching in Half Moon Bay, so they called her. She rushed home. I was rushed to the hospital where they pumped my stomach. After the ER visit, an ambulance took me to a psych ward in South San Francisco. When we entered, I saw people that I did not want to be around. I demanded they let me out. Mary didn't agree but took me home. Mary informed my computer company what was going on, and at that point, I was put on medical leave. The psychologist and my family doctor sent written reports to my company on my medical condition, and they requested I see the company doctor, which I did. Whenever I started talking, I started to cry. I spent about ten minutes crying with the company doctor, and he supported the position of my doctors. My life was a mess, and all I wanted to do was to die. No control and scared to death, I felt like I had let my family and my wife down. I wasn't able to provide the stability that Eric, JJ, and Mary required.

I stayed on medical leave off and on until I retired from my company. We decided to use our company moving-and-living-expenses benefit and started looking for a new home to reduce our financial issues. We decided to buy a home in Discovery Bay, California. This didn't meet my company's guidelines, but I didn't care. Let them do something.

To get away from the situation, Mary and I met friends from New Jersey in San Antonio, Texas. They were our best friends, and he had also been on corporate staff. We went there to spend New Year's Eve and to get me away from all the things that reminded me of how badly the company had treated me. In Texas, I started relaxing and felt like I had the support of real friends and Mary. It was the start to recovery, and they did their best to help me put the matter behind me.

We made a reservation for dinner at San Franciscan Restaurant in San Antonio for 9:00 p.m. It was in the middle of San Antonio at the river walk, and it was famous for New Year's Eve. Well, 9:00 p.m. came and went, and they kept calling large groups but not a foursome. I went up many times to ask when we would be able to be seated. They finally informed me that they were only taking large groups. I came up with a plan. We should form a *large* group! It was about ten thirty. We were hungry, and lots of people were waiting. My marketing skills went into action. I went around the room explaining to couples that they were only taking large groups and asked if they would like to join my group. It was easy, and quickly I got the necessary people. I went back to the front desk and told them I had the group and if they would please call us soon. Yes, they called us next, and we then had a table in the restaurant, thirteen people. We had no idea who the others were, so I became head of the table. We went around the table, and each introduced themselves and where they lived.

This made me feel great; I hadn't lost my skills. I will say I believe we all had a great New Year's Eve party with people we had never met before.

By January 1993, we were six months from JJ's graduation, and we were in the process of buying a new home. Our Half Moon Bay house sold quickly with a hefty profit, and we needed to be out by April 1. We bought a home in Discovery Bay, California, and our furniture was moved to our new home. During this time, we needed to be close to Half Moon Bay. JJ would be graduating from high school, and Mary was still substituting there. Sometimes I was driving to San Jose. We lived in a temporary apartment in Foster City.

While waiting for JJ to graduate, we did things to the new home on the weekends that needed to be done because the house had been in in foreclosure. We bought it straight from the bank, and Mary did a great job reducing the price, allowing us an opportunity to survive. We then were living in Discovery Bay.

1993–2004

Discovery Bay, California

In Discovery Bay, I was still working for my company in a job I hated, and my feelings were anything but positive. And I was cleared by the doctors to go back to work.

I went back to the San Jose plant to work, and the pressure started building again. One day while at home, I started having very severe pains on the side my heart is located. Mary arrived with our daughter, who had just had our first grandson. As they walked in, I was grabbing my chest and curling up. Mary rushed me to the first clinic she saw. We were so new to the area we didn't have a doctor. The doctor gave me Demerol and waited until he was sure I could make it to the hospital. Then we went on our way. He had called a heart specialist who met us at the ER, and they rushed me into the ICU. I spent two days while they ran many tests. They found that I had had a stress heart attack, and now the lower left side of my heart was dead. Once they had me stabilized, I was released.

My guardian angel was working on my behalf again because my division announced another "window" for retirement, and the term of this window allowed me to retire with full benefits. I got two weeks' pay for every year of service, which was twenty-nine years by that time; 110 days of vacation pay; and medical for the rest of my life. They allowed their employees to have a five-year window, but I only needed a few months. I signed the papers in March of 1994 and received my severance money. I did have to wait for a few months to get retirement because it was a few months my start date, September 1968.

I then spent some time just relaxing at home for a while, not worrying about work. Mary felt I should wait until I completely recovered before I started looking for another job. Mary was substitute teaching in the Discovery Bay area while I became the housekeeper. Believe me—I had no idea what I was getting into. That job was hard and not fun. Mary did reprimand me about the laundry, however. She was not happy with the whites. She told me there were three types of whites and you don't wash them all together. Boy, did I get my act together and start separating them into three piles.

That summer, JJ graduated and moved in with us while going to Delta College and playing football. Eric finished his freshman year at Sonoma State. He got a job for the summer at the boat docks in Discovery Bay, helping people put their boats in and out of the water plus pumping gas for boats as needed.

One of the things I did enjoy was golfing with my cousin by marriage. Each year, we took two weeks and traveled the Northwest playing golf. On one of our trips, I could tell my cousin was not happy.

Finally, after a round of golf, while we were having a beer prior to leaving, he looked at me and said, "I need to tell you something."

I said, "Sure, what is the problem?"

He informed me my father-in-law had sexually abused his wife. I was shocked! I told him that couldn't be true. He said it was very hard on him since he was like a father to him. I asked him what he was going to do. He said he confronted my father-in-law about what his wife had said, and he denied it ever happened. He didn't know whether to believe his wife or his father-in-law.

I told my cousin I'd look into it, but he asked me not to. I told him I was aware that he had had an affair with a woman when they lived in Benicia, but I found it very hard to believe he would do that kind of thing with family. I asked him if I had his permission to discuss with my wife, and he said no problem. I also asked what he was going to do about it, and he said his wife didn't want anything done and he was going to honor her request.

When I got home from the two-week trip a few days later, I told my wife what he had said; and for some reason, she believed it could have happened. She would not tell me why but assured me it most likely was true.

Life went on, and one more time, my guardian angel came to my rescue since I didn't like this housekeeping. I got a call from my former company asking if I would be willing to come back to work under contract. I told them I had to think about it and asked them to call me back in a couple of days. They did; and I told them I would under three conditions: One, I received the same amount of pay I was receiving while working for them. Two, I wanted to work from home; and three, I wanted to choose the jobs I wanted to work on. Well, guess what, they said okay! I went back to work and out of that housekeeping job.

I worked under those conditions for three years. Then our favorite agency in the United States government, the IRS, got involved. They informed my company that they had to either cut me or make me an employee. I told them there was no way was I coming back, so I left. During that time with my company, I became good friends with a gentleman who was the CEO and owner of an enterprise management consultant and implementation firm. Their headquarters was located in Pasadena, California, and he offered me a job as vice president of worldwide consulting and implementation for the firm. I took the job and was with them for another few years until my son Eric graduated from college.

One evening, after Mary and I had gone to bed, the phone rang. Since the phone was on her side of the bed, she answered the phone and had a long conversation. I could tell it was important because she was just listening to the person and wasn't talking much. Finally she told the person to discuss with her husband, and she handed me the phone. I looked at her and asked what it was about.

She didn't say a word, so I said, "Can I help you?"

The young man on the other end of the phone told me he believed I was his birth father. Now I will tell you that woke me up in a hurry! I asked who he was and why he believed that. He told me he found his birth mother, and she had told me that I was his father. I asked who his birth mother was, and he told me the name of that young lady I had caught in bed with her brother's best friend.

He asked me how many years I had been married, and I had to ask Mary. She said over thirty years. He told me his birth mother was a dentist in St. Louis and had been married three different times.

Yes, it was the same woman that I had been with and felt it was time to clear the matter up once and for all. I told the young man what had happened—about her meetings with my pastor at the time and what he told me. I also told him I would be willing to take a DNA to make sure he was or wasn't my child.

The best he could tell me about his mother was that she was a mess. I knew this young lady came from a very well-to-do family and her father was a very rich doctor. She was the oldest of the family who had everything she ever wanted. But when she got pregnant, her father kicked her out, and she was on her own. I told the young man what I knew, and he informed me that her dad had sent her to a home in Oregon to have the baby (this young man) and he paid for her to finish her education and become a dentist. He also informed me that she put him up for adoption and never saw him again.

With that, I decided to tell him the details of the situation. At that time, his mother was in her early twenties. The young man was her brother's best friend, and he was around sixteen. She told him my name so she didn't have to admit she had had sex with a minor. I told him to contact me if he would like me to take the paternity test. I have never heard from him again since.

In that same time frame, another tragedy happened in my life. Dad passed away in the summer of 1995. This was very hard on me because he had always been very special to me. I believe that one of the reasons I was with the Woodwards and never was allowed to leave is the fact that Dad never had any children of his own. I believe the reason they wanted me was so Dad and Mom could look at each other and know that I was adopted by both. I never heard Dad say anything about sending me back. In fact, I know he was never around when mother made statements about what a mistake it was to keep me. I never asked him; but I do know that, when I was fifteen and Mother told me about the move to California, he was at work. I am not sure what his reaction would have been if he had heard the words she used. I can tell you this: I was always his son. When he had the time, he took me places. He also bought me a horse and a bike. At the time of Mother's death, he made it very clear to Bob and Shirley I was in charge. He was a very special dad and at times a father, working to support his family.

After Mother's death, Dad had been living in a mobile home park, and I had taken over all financial transactions for him. He looked to me to take care of him. As the years went by, his health got worse to the point that he had dementia. And soon we needed to put him in a home. I wanted, in the worst way, to have him live with us. But he had become dangerous, and as I was traveling a lot, it would not be wise to leave him with Mary. So he was put in a home, and eventually he decided to starve himself to death. He wouldn't eat. He had previously signed a document stating he wanted no life-sustaining care. It was tough because, each week, the home would call, asking to put him on liquid feeding; and I kept saying no. His doctor from Kaiser and I were in total agreement, but the fact we were allowing Dad to starve himself to death was very tough.

As his time came closer, I still felt guilty, and I remember the last time I saw him alive. He wasn't doing very well. I knew his time wasn't long, but I needed to go home to my family. I had called his pastor who lived in the area and asked him if he would come see Dad. He came in a heartbeat, which made me feel good. But while I was at home, he passed away, and I didn't make it back in time. I will never be able to get over the guilt for not being there in the last moments for the dad/father who took me in, gave me a home, and loved me with all his heart. I believe to this day that I was his real child, as real as you can be. He was ninety-three, and allowing him to join Mother seemed like a good thing. This poem expresses my true feeling:

> You never said I'm leaving.
> You never said goodbye.
> You were gone before I knew it,
> and God knows why.
> In life I loved you dearly.
> In death I love you still.
> In my heart I hold a place,
> that only you can fill.
> It broke my heart to lose you,
> but you didn't go alone.
> A part of me went with you,
> the day God took you home.
> (Took quote from a gravestone in Ireland)

In 1996, Eric graduated from college. As a present, Mary and I wanted to take him to Europe. The only one problem was that he was in love with a young lady whom he was dating and who graduated with him. We decided to take both as a reward. In addition, he informed us he was going to ask her to marry him on the trip. I'm not sure how this happened to this day, but his best friend and brother somehow weaseled his way to join us. Yes, JJ was going to be along on Eric's graduation trip. Maybe it was in case that the young lady said no, so he would be there to support his brother.

Off we went to Paris, France, where our godson from England, Geoff, was supposed to be waiting for us when we arrived. I had, however, given him the name of the wrong hotel. As a result, he drove us from the airport to the wrong hotel. Off we went on a bus, and then we changed to the underground. And through all this, we had all our luggage; and Jen, Eric's girlfriend, had gotten sick on the flight and still wasn't feeling well.

We finally arrived at the correct hotel, and Geoff was ready to show us Paris. Now remember we hadn't slept and were very tired. So off we went to visit a few places that afternoon. When it was time for dinner, Geoff had arranged a wonderful dinner at an Italian restaurant in Paris with singing waiters. We had a very nice dinner and convinced Geoff we all had to get some sleep. We were wrong—not JJ! He wanted to go drinking with Geoff, so off they went. We agreed to meet at nine the next morning at Notre Dame Cathedral.

Eric, Jen, Mary, and I attended the eight o'clock Mass and then met Geoff and JJ outside. When we saw them, they didn't look too good. They had a tough night, but it was a great story. JJ and Geoff had gone to a pub for a few beers, and while they were sitting at the bar, a young lady kept coming up and asking JJ if he would like to buy flowers. He kept saying no, but she wouldn't give up. Finally JJ asked her why she was insisting that he buy flowers.

She said, "For your boyfriend."

He said, "What? He isn't my lover! Why do you think that?"

All guys in France who shave their head and wear a beard are gay. He assured her he wasn't gay and neither was Geoff. He told her he was from California in the United States. As I understand it, she called a friend, and the four of them sat and drank together.

Geoff was going back to England that afternoon, so we all decided to go to the Palace of Versailles. Off on the train we went. The little town outside the palace had a market in the center, and we walked around town and ate lunch. Geoff spent the morning with us and then headed back to England through the Chunnel.

We have another comical story concerning our son JJ. At the palace, Mary liked reading all the signs explaining each room, and so did Eric and Jen. I knew this and headed down the hall to find a place to sit and wait. I liked looking at the rooms, but I wasn't going to read about them. After a minute, I saw JJ walking toward me.

He said, "This is stupid! I am not interested in reading all this crap!"

I laughed told him to sit down and watch the people going by.

We were sitting there when suddenly JJ hit me and said, "Dad, those girls are looking at me!"

I turned to see them, and JJ had already joined them and was taking their picture with their camera.

For someone who didn't like this thing, JJ became the tour guide for these two ladies. I am sure they didn't know I was his dad, so I got up to follow and listen to JJ trying to impress these young ladies with his knowledge of the palace. It was really funny to listen to.

As he was looking at a large bedroom on display, he said to the two, "I know what I would do with this room!"

It was Mary's birthday, and we all went out for her birthday dinner on that most popular street in Paris—you know the one. We were eating dinner when JJ got up and said he had to go. I looked at him and asked him where he was going. He told us that he was meeting those two young ladies at a pub in Paris. I asked him where, and he told me the name of the pub but didn't know where it was. Off he went, and the rest of us finished dinner followed by a cruise down the Seine River.

After the cruise, we headed for the Hard Rock Café in Paris to have a hot fudge sundae. It was about eleven at night, and Jen and Eric decided they were tired. Jen was still not feeling well, so they went to the hotel to sleep.

Mary and I sat there with our sundaes, enjoying the time together alone. I should tell you that Eric had informed us that he had an engagement ring and was going to ask Jen to marry him someplace on our trip. He had the ring in his backpack, and it was making Mother and me very nervous. We both wished he would give it to Jen in Paris and get it over with. We finished our sundaes and walked out of the Hard Rock Café to go to the hotel.

We were walking down the street when I saw a guy walking down the middle of the street around 1:00 a.m. The closer we got to him, the more I realized it was our son JJ. He was sure glad to see us! He had forgotten which hotel we were staying in and didn't know where to go. A guy who could find a pub with those girls couldn't find his own hotel! This was going to be interesting vacation.

The next morning, we got up—everyone except JJ. He had no intent of going to any museum, and he said he would meet us at noon. Eric, Jen, Mary, and I headed to the Louvre Museum; but I was wishing I was still in bed like JJ. We arrived at the museum. I warned Eric and Jen that Mary liked to spend a long time looking at things, but they told me no problem. They liked to look also and wanted to go with Mary. I told them I was going down the hall to find a place to sit and wait for them.

After about thirty minutes, Eric came rushing up to me and said, "Help! Mother is driving us nuts! She takes so long on each piece."

I laughed and got up to follow him. When we found Mary, I asked her if I could talk to her. I told her we couldn't be there all day because we had to meet JJ and go to the Eiffel Tower. After that, she went much faster and made us all happy. I was only interested in seeing the Mona Lisa painting.

Then off we went to the Eiffel Tower. When we arrived, it was raining. Up we went to the top. I hoped Eric was going to ask Jen to marry him at the top, but he didn't. One thing I do remember was that, when we looked at the clouds moving overhead, if we watched too long, it felt like the tower was swaying. We decided to head down and got on the elevator. It was supposed to stop halfway down, and as we got to that halfway point, the operator tried to stop it. The cable was wet and greasy, and we slid right by. Now the question was, What would happen when we got to the bottom? No problem, the operator started stopping prior to the spot, and we slid right to proper spot.

We had a great time and enjoyed every minute. The next morning, we picked up the van at the airport and headed for Switzerland and Italy. Eric still had that ring, and we all wanted him to put it on her hand before he lost it.

We had an extra day, and I had a great idea. "Let's head for Titisee, Germany."

This is my favorite location in Europe, and Eric knew this. It is a little village in the Black Forest of Germany where the Black Forest cake was invented. We stayed in a cabin where there was no TV and no phone. After dinner, Eric said he and Jen were going to take a walk. I looked at Mary with a smile, and I was right. He took her down to the little lake, and at the boat dock, he asked her to marry him.

Yep, you're correct—she accepted. Now we had a problem. She wanted to call all her family to tell them. We had no phone in the room, and believe it or not, we didn't even know what a cell phone was back then. We went to the pay phone across the street. Some of you may not know what that is. I took out my phone credit card, and she made those phone calls. I will say it may have been cheaper for me to have bought the engagement ring.

The ring was no longer a worry. We were off to Lucerne to see the famous covered bridge and look around the town before heading to Interlaken, Switzerland, one of the spots that Mary and I wanted the kids to see before we arrived in Italy. When we arrived, we only had one place we wanted to see—the restaurant on top of the Swiss Alps. We needed to take six trams/gondolas to get up to it. We did it and had breakfast at the restaurant. Mary put her purse on the windowsill. After a while, it wasn't there anymore, and we had to go find it. We discovered the windowsill was moving around the restaurant and we were standing still!

When we came down the mountain, JJ saw the ideal thing that he wanted to do on his European trip. He wanted to do a 480-meter bungee jump from a gondola. Mary, Jen, and I stood there as our son did that jump. Eric was not there because he wasn't feeling well and wanted to take a nap. Don't believe that for a minute. If he went with us, JJ would make him do the jump, and that was not his cup of tea.

On our way to Italy, the ladies wanted to drive along a road along the ocean, like Highway 1 in California. That was a day I will never forget because the drive was really bad on the winding road, but we arrived at the small village of Portofino. Everyone was tired, so we stopped in town and asked where we could stay. People arranged a reservation for us at the Hotel Porto Roca. But how to find it? We headed up the only street we could drive, and sure enough, we were headed out of town. I saw a person and asked where the hotel was, and he told us we had to park in the city parking lot and the hotel was about one mile up the hill. Thank God, Eric and JJ were with us! As we were walking toward the hotel, the two women had to look at the shops, and JJ was looking at the beach. He grabbed me and pointed to a woman lying in the sun. Yes, they all had no tops on. I could tell another story about JJ and the beach but will just say he had a great time. We left Portofino and headed for Rome.

We did make a stop at the Leaning Tower of Pisa, and this was an interesting stop. We parked on a side street, and on the way to the tower, we passed many vendors. It looked like this place was a big moneymaker. We all went into the tower but not to the top, and we were there about an hour. I was not really impressed with the tower. It would be fun to see it fall—maybe on Halloween night, I could make that happen.

We continued on to Rome where we spent about three days, but I was ready to leave after one day. After that, we took a train from Naples to the ruins of Pompeii and had some great fun. As we walked through this place, we found it so sad but interesting to see remains still in the place from when the volcano erupted in AD 80.

That was the end of our memorable trip, and we returned to the United States. Eric needed to find a real full-time job; so I talked to Rick, my boss in Pasadena, about hiring him into his business. So at that point, Eric started working with me, and then off to school he went in San Diego to learn programming from a network management firm.

It was clear within a short period of time that Eric needed me to leave the company so he could make his own path. He didn't need Dad watching over him and giving him advice. Rick and I talked about the situation, and the decision was for me to leave.

I left my friend's company and found work with a consulting company as senior consultant in enterprise management. I reported to a partner of the company, a Frenchman working in New York City who had no integrity. About three months into the job, I couldn't take it any longer and told Mary I was just going to sit home and play golf and see how long it takes them to realize I wasn't working. And I did just that. Around the first of the year, I got a call from my boss asking what I was doing.

I said, "Nothing."

He asked me why not, and I told him I was not working for a company that lied to the customers and sent consultants who had no idea what they were doing.

My boss asked me to meet him in Los Angeles at the Admirals Club at LAX, and I did. In the meeting, he asked me why I didn't just quit. I asked him why I should quit when they were paying me six figures. Did he think I was dumb? He then told me he needed to put me on an improvement program for ninety days. I was fine with that, but after ninety days, I still had not done a thing. They then terminated me, but I was able to collect unemployment for a year.

Mary, meanwhile, had gone back to school and had gotten her teaching credential. I decided to change my career direction, and I took the CBEST test in California to become a substitute teacher. I passed and started substitute teaching in Tracy, California, and Mary was teaching fifth grade at a private school. It wasn't long before I got a phone call from Mary's principal. She needed my help and wondered if I would be interested in teaching the sixth grade full-time. It seemed that the teacher was not working out.

Teaching was going to be my new profession. The class was a mess, and her gradebook was too. I taught the rest of that year and then moved up to teach seventh-grade history, computers, seventh-grade math, and eighth-grade history. It was fun, but the pay was not that great. In fact, it was bad. I did two more years teaching at the school and then didn't want to do it anymore. Once again, I didn't like being inside all day. At least I had a new class every fifty minutes and great kids who wanted to learn.

The next major event was the marriage of our son Eric—the one who got engaged in Germany on his graduation adventure. My wonderful wife, Mary, was asked to make the wedding dress. Jen and Eric set the wedding date on December 5, 1999, and Mary was very busy making a wedding dress while still teaching school.

Our son was about to take a very important step in his life. The night before the wedding, at the hotel, Mary somehow created a *big* problem with the veil. It wasn't pretty. Mary had to iron the veil, and since the hotel didn't supply irons, she had to make a trip to the local Walmart. She got back and, while ironing the veil, melted some of the tulle. What to do? Quickly she called her cousin Vicky to help her out of this mess. I had already gone to bed when Vicky showed up, and between the two of them, they decided they needed to go back to the store to buy some invisible thread. It was really late, and thank goodness the store stayed open late. It wasn't long before they had repaired the veil, and no one ever knew what happened. The wedding was great, and now we had another person added to the family.

Eric and Jen moved to Pasadena where Eric kept his job, and Jen got a job at a large department store. She got pregnant right away, so they both wanted to move closer to their families. Eric was offered a job with a telecommunication company and accepted it. That allowed them to move back to the Bay Area. Jen and Eric moved to Benicia, California; and shortly after, Jen gave birth to a really big boy, Brady—eleven pounds, seven ounces—and later to a very beautiful baby girl, Brinkley. Jen and Eric have since divorced, but at least they are still friends. Eric lives in Manteca, California, and Jen lives in Tamales, California. She has the two kids during the week, and Eric has them on weekends.

As you remember, back in 1975, my father-in-law and I had become very close because he and his son had a problem between them because of his son's wife. Whenever my father-in-law needed to go to the doctor or hospital, he wanted me there. We took long walks together and talked about life and things we were going through. We went to ballgames together and on vacation together; and for sure, when he needed help or I needed help, we went to each other. I took total care of him. When he died, his son did not arrive until the night before the funeral. The funeral arrangements and the service were held at their church, where he was on the board, in Red Bluff, California.

I had to go back home after the funeral and teach the next day, but Mary decided to stay with her mother for a few days. Mary and several relatives decided to go bowling. Mary is a very good bowler. I'm not sure if she was showing off or just unlucky, but the first time she went to the line to throw the ball, she slipped and fell. Everyone followed her to the hospital. Mary broke her wrist badly, and the party was over.

Yes, those days on the Walnut Ranch in Red Bluff where my in-laws lived were very special for our kids. They loved driving the tractor and playing in the walnut orchard. After Dad passed away, I became in charge of my mother-in-law, and it wasn't easy. She wanted to give money to everyone who called, and I had to put an end to that. That meant I was on her bank account so I could watch what she was doing. I recovered some of the money she gave away. She did very well for several years.

A few months later, Mary told me something that hit me like a bolt of lightning. Mary told me something that had been a secret for the past twenty years. Had I known, there would have been some major changes in our family. I am sure that is why she didn't tell me. She said she was sexually assaulted by her father.

I said, "What?"

She had tears in her eyes and repeated the information. I asked her when that happened, and she told me it was when we lived in Half Moon Bay.

Once again, I was questioning the true meaning of love, and the hurt went to the bottom of my soul. One more time, in my mind, I was reliving November of 1956. The three things I put forward back then were control of my life, enough money so no one could hurt me, and the love that was missing in my life. Then she informed me the same thing happened between her and her ear, nose, and throat doctor who did surgery on her nasal passage. I asked her why she didn't tell me about it; and the answer was that, anytime she went to see him after that, she made sure my daughter was always with her.

I was very crushed and angry. Over the years, I learned that Mary never wanted to be part of anything that may cause problems and also wanted no one except me to be mad at her. Many times, she avoided the truth when it could cause those involved to think badly of her. In our many years of marriage, it was clear to me, if it came down to a disagreement between myself and another person, I could count on her taking the position of the other person and, for sure, our children. I also finally understood why she said she believed her cousin when she claimed her father had molested her.

This was not the first time Mary had kept things from me that any husband has the right to know. I once found out at dinner Dad was not the birth father of Mom's two children. I was about twenty-eight or twenty-nine years of age, and on the way home from that dinner, Mary told me she already knew because my sister-in-law had told her right after our marriage.

The second thing she finally told me something that I needed to know was that my mom had come to her shortly after our marriage and told her, if she wanted to get a divorce, she would understand. I was in my sixties when she informed me of this, after Mom had died.

I could go on about others, but these are just three examples of secrets in the relationship between my wife and me. For me, the revelation about her father was the straw that broke the camel's back. The more I thought about this situation, the less rational I got. What was marriage? Couldn't I find someone in the world who would be honest with me and love me as God so instructed in those wedding vows? What about His message to all Christians that God comes first, husband or wife second, family third, and the rest of the world next? I guessed I was in that last group and hit rock bottom. She would rather hurt me than another people. I gave serious thought about divorce; but I had taken wedding vows that, under God and witnesses, I was required to keep.

Now what you are going to read will be something that any man who wants to keep those vows and still loves his family should never have done. I have no idea what I was thinking. But my wife kept secrets from me, so in my mind, I did the same to get back and satisfy my ego. My mind never thought that I was violating one of the Ten Commandments. I decided to have sexual relations; I guess to get even because of Mary not telling me about sexual assault she had been through.

I didn't want an affair, nor did I want to cause major problems to my marriage as I felt it would ruin my life and again put me back into the state where I felt no one wanted me. But my hate for my father-in-law and my hurt for my wife not being honest to me for twenty-some years was too much.

I did something that no man who loves his wife should do. Why I did it, I didn't understand, but the anger and with my wife and the hate for my father-in-law started a process I am not proud of. I cheated on my wedding vows and my wife and knew it was wrong, but anger and hate were in control. Did I do it for sexual pleasure?

No. I was just hurt in a very major way. I had no personal interest in an affair.

Mary's father sexually abused her, and she didn't tell me until twenty-two years later. Her doctor sexually abused her, and again she never told me.

Was I ashamed of what I did? I was and, over time, knew I could not keep doing what I was doing. I knew, if I told Mary, I would lose her; and my life would be over. I had to learn to live with the situation and hope that what I had done would never come to her attention. One of the things God gave me was the ability to just stop if I didn't want to do it any longer. I had done that with smoking and with musical instruments, and now I did it with my sexual life.

One Sunday morning in October, Mary received a phone call from her cousin Vicky that her husband, Steve, had passed away with a heart attack. He had just turned fifty and was very high up in the Department of Forestry. A little later, she received another call from his sister asking if I would be willing to go down and assist Vicky with the funeral arrangements. I agreed and left that afternoon for our cousin's home, only to arrive to a very depressing situation.

I asked Vicky to join me on the back porch to get away from the other people and asked her what happened. In that conversation, she asked me to take over all responsibility for the arrangements as she wanted a full-honor funeral that had been offered to her by the Department of Forestry.

I had worked in the morgue at a hospital while in college and had overseen the funeral arrangements of some six or seven people, but I had never been in charge of something like this. Where to start? The first thing to do was to meet with the Department of Forestry to understand what they had in mind. It was decided that they would take care of the traffic control over the area as the funeral moved from the church to the cemetery. They were going to have a formal parade. They would also be in charge of the honor guard for the wake and the funeral, and they would also take care of all the arrangements necessary for the people after the funeral and cemetery service. There were going to be regional fire chiefs, the police department, fire station representatives from all over the state, and the secretary of state. Along with these people was the equipment that CFD used to fight fires.

Now I understood I just had to find a place that would accommodate around three hundred dignitaries from all over the state, plus all the friends and family. This was going to be interesting as it was going to be held in the small town of Paso Robles, California.

Some of my responsibilities included getting Steve out of the coroner's office, handling all the relatives, and keeping the funeral home apprised of everything that was taking place. Plus I needed to attend all meetings for the family. They wanted the funeral on the upcoming Saturday.

I sat down with the regional fire chief of the area and wanted to understand why they hadn't found his heart problem when they gave him his physical just prior to the last major fire which he was in charge of in the Los Angeles area. It was fortunate that Steve had turned fifty just a few weeks prior to his heart attack because Vicky would now receive 80 percent of his salary for the rest of her life. If it had happened during a fire, she would have received 100 percent.

My first challenge was finding a place to have the funeral. I started looking, and all the churches were way too small except for a Baptist church in Paso Robles. Steve did not believe in God and had no church affiliation, so this could have caused a problem. Mary and I were attending a large Baptist church in Stockton, California, at the time; so I set up a meeting with the Paso Robles pastor, sat down, and told him what was going on. I told him we needed his church for the Saturday morning funeral. I informed him that we would cover all costs plus we would need some of the church staff present in case of problems and also for running the communication system. He told me he would take it up with the church board and get back to me. It was Tuesday, and he would call the board together for the meeting that evening.

The next important thing had to be arranged ASAP. Vicky told me they did not have a grave and didn't know what to do.

I told her, "Let's take care of that problem."

So off we went to the only cemetery in Paso Robles, very nice and quite large. I found out it was the main cemetery for the county.

Vicky and I sat down with a young lady to purchase a gravesite for the two of them. That was very easy although very tense. But then we had a problem. When I told the young lady that the funeral was on Saturday, she looked at me and said the cemetery was not open on Saturdays. This shook Vicky up. I told her to not worry and to trust me. We paid for both graves and left. I took Vicky home and told her I needed to do some things.

I headed back to the cemetery and met with the young lady again. We continued to discuss having the funeral on Saturday, but I was not getting anywhere. So I played a trump card. I told her it would be on Saturday and, if they had a problem, I would be in touch with the necessary people in the state who would be attending the funeral. If the cemetery didn't approve the Saturday funeral by 10:00 a.m. Wednesday, I would contact the state officials on Wednesday afternoon. When Wednesday came, I got the call that they would be open for the funeral.

The next item was to get the body from the coroner's office to the funeral home. I was able to achieve that on Wednesday. After the body was at the funeral home, I took Vicky and her son Michael to the funeral home to make the arrangements. Everything went very well, and when we were about to go in and choose a casket, I asked to speak to Vicky and Michael alone. I warned them that, when they walked into that room, the reality of the situation could have a major effect on them. This would be their first time choosing the casket that Steve would be in forever, and they would never see him again after the lid was closed. Vicky was so glad I reviewed this with her, and she was able to handle the situation.

On Thursday, I learned that one of their children was not going to be able to attend the funeral. At this point, I need to say that he was Vicky's child from a prior marriage and Steve had adopted him. He had become a Mormon, was on his mission trip in Peru, and would not come home. This upset Vicky to no end, and I spent the day trying to change his mind by phone. No matter what pressure I brought on the local Mormon church, they were steadfast that he should stay on his mission.

Friday came, and it was time to set up for the Friday night viewing. I told the funeral home that I wanted to view Steve that afternoon. They asked why, and I told them I wanted to make sure it looked like Steve, remembering when Mom and I saw Grandma Woodward. The time came; and I took Michael, who was eighteen, to the funeral home. We viewed the body, and I asked Michael if it looked like Steve. He looked at me and said not really. I asked what the problem was, and he told me his neck was way too large.

I looked at the funeral director and said, "We need to change that."

"I don't know what to do to change it," he said.

I said, "Could we loosen the shirt so it would not be so pushed forward?"

He said he could cut the collar, but he didn't have anyone there at present who could assist.

I said, "Yes, you do. You have me!"

With that, I asked Michael to leave. The funeral director got some tin snips. I reached over and pulled Charles's body against mine, and he cut the collar. I laid him back down, and sure enough, it smoothed out his neck. I brought Michael back in.

When he looked, he said, "Yes, that is my father."

The rest of the funeral arrangements went off without a hitch, and I was very pleased. I was even able to arrange for the small children who would be attending to get a ride on the firetrucks from the cemetery to the church. The regional director of the Department of Forestry told me I would make one heck of a crisis manager.

After the funeral, I had one more thing to do. I was not convinced that Steve had had a heart attack for no reason, so I talked to Vicky about what I wanted to do. She was okay with what I had in mind. I asked around and found the number-one pathologist in the state of California, and I contacted him. He assured me that he could look at the biopsied heart tissues and tell us if the fatal heart attack was that Sunday or if he had had another prior attack which was the fatal one. We flew him from Sacramento to Paso Robles to review the local pathologist's findings and also do his own chemical tests on the tissue.

Two days later, he got back to me and told me the exact date and time that Steve had the first heart attack which caused the fatal one. That date and time was while Steve was working on a fire months before. Because he didn't want to be in charge of the current fire, he was working the fire line with the other firefighters. These findings were presented to the proper people, and Vicky's benefit moved from 80 percent to 100 percent of his pay. In addition, her two sons would get full tuition to the state college or university of their choice in California.

In 2004, it was clear I wanted to leave the scene of my adultery, and Mary was tired of the heat and boat living. Because the real estate market was on the rise, we decided we should sell our home. And she wanted to move to the mountains and build the home of her dreams. Our decision in May of 2004 was to build a home in Pine Grove, California. As I was the contractor of the home in Moss Beach, I could do the same thing for this home. We would hang onto our home in Discovery Bay for a bit, buy a motor home to live in at the new place, and put the bad memories in Discovery Bay behind me.

2004–2018

Pine Grove, California

We bought a one-acre property in Pine Grove and started the process of building Mary's dream home, which she designed. We started the job in May of 2004 and were to finish in November. I hired my nephew from Idaho because he had built our house in Moss Beach, and with him, he brought his partner to assist in the job. I had never met this person, but my nephew assured me he was as dedicated as the guys he used to build my home in Moss Beach. As contractor, I knew I would have to hire other subcontractors as needed. This gave me something to do and some time off from teaching. We broke ground on May 4, 2004. My nephew and his partner were living in his partner's trailer they brought.

In June, his partner's wife came to spend the summer in their trailer. Mary had finished school, so she moved up to the new location. I had made arrangements with a neighbor to use their mobile home for Mary and me to stay in, about one-fourth mile away and on another street. At the first part of June, my nephew had no place to stay nor anyone to be around after work when the workday was over. As I had made arrangements with the neighbor, my nephew moved into the motor home where I had been staying.

During this time, we were trying to sell our home in Discovery Bay. It was a seller's market, but our price range was very hard to sell. I started feeling depressed again because I wasn't in control and about to run out of money to finish our new home.

At the first of October, I needed to get a new foreman and crew as my nephew's crew was required to go home. This caused problems with the job. We were running behind. It was the first of October, and they had been there since May of that year. I had a new contractor to oversee the project, and he wanted to use his people to finish the house. I agreed because we had sold our home in Discovery Bay. The new contractor installed Sheetrock and the plumbing/electricity. I insisted on keeping him to finish the job because he was a personal friend, and he agreed.

Now it was time to install the cabinets in the kitchen and three bathrooms. At the beginning of the job, my nephew wanted to use his cabinetmaker; so he came down, took measurements, and gave me a quote, of which Mary and I approved. That was why, way back in June, we knew we were going to need them installed by or around September or October. Now that my nephew had left, my new contractor said we needed them in two weeks. The original cost of the house included custom cabinets for the kitchen and three bathrooms, so I called the cabinetmaker to come install them. He said he didn't have the time and that I could come get them in Idaho. I said the contract included having him do the installation. What do I do? Discussing this with my wife, we decided to go and get the cabinets in Idaho because the present crew was good and could do the installation.

Then I had a new task. I called my cousin in Red Bluff and asked what he was doing. He said he wasn't doing anything. I asked him if he would be willing to go with me to Idaho and assist me in getting the cabinets. I told him I would take care of all costs; I just wanted help to load and drive the truck back. We had an agreement, and he said could be ready to go that afternoon. I arranged the tickets for the two of us to fly from California to Idaho where we rented a one-way truck to bring the cabinets back to California.

The next day, we headed to Idaho and arrived late in the afternoon. We got transportation from the airport to the truck rental company and rented the truck. Because it was late afternoon by then, we decided to wait until the next day to go get the cabinets. The next morning, we headed to the building center, and when we arrived, I got the surprise of my life. He had built the special cabinets my wife had asked for, but he said he did not have the time to build the custom cabinets.

He had normal cabinets that would fit in the kitchen but none for the three bathrooms. With that, I said we needed to adjust the price. He told me no and, if I wanted them, I had to pay the price agreed upon. I now knew what my nephew was going to do to get even. Here I was in Idaho, finding out for the first time that his cabinetmaker was not going to honor the agreement. It was also clear he didn't care. My cousin got hot and started to give him a piece of his mind, but I stopped that quick. I paid him what we agreed, and we were told we had to load them ourselves. We loaded the truck, and at least he allowed us to use his dolly to load the truck. We left in the late afternoon, and each drove one-hour shifts to arrive back home the next morning. The crew on-site unloaded the truck. My new contractor noticed they weren't custom cabinets.

I said, "I know, but just install, please."

I also needed to find cabinets for the three bathrooms, get them here, and have them installed so the plumbing could be finished.

Mary and I had to find the necessary cabinets fast for the three bathrooms. I can also tell you at this time the doctor decided to increase my depression medication so I didn't go into depression again as I had two prior times. I asked our contractor how soon he needed the new cabinets and was informed in the next week or so. Off we went, found them, paid for them, and had them delivered, all within one week.

Sometime in October, I received an invoice from the lumber company in Idaho, plus a letter from the owner of the company telling me I owed $10,000 for the product. I made a phone call to that person, and we had a very interesting chat. First I informed him that I believe he had no document with my signature ordering the material. Second I had a whole lot of material at the jobsite, and if they wanted to come get it, they could have it. I informed him I was not going to pay the $10,000 as that was my nephew's account and he would have to take it up with him.

I explained to the owner that my nephew told me he needed to leave the first of August and they would be back when the siding came in as he couldn't do any more work until the siding for the house arrived. The owner informed me that the siding had been sitting in the lumberyard since the first of July and wondered why we hadn't asked for it to be shipped. This was the first time I was aware that my nephew had outright lied to me and Mary.

We moved in at Thanksgiving 2004. The whole family came to spend the holiday in our new home, and it was great to have the family together. Mary proved to me that we could house all our kids and their families in this one home. At this time, we only had five grandchildren, three married children, and JJ.

Fortieth Anniversary

2005

A major event occurred shortly after we moved into our new home. In August 2005, we celebrated our fortieth wedding anniversary. Now tell me how anyone could put up with me for forty years! Remember that kid in England who we call our foster son, Geoff? He talked to Mary because he had always wanted us to go to Zimbabwe where he was born. It wasn't hard for him to sell that deal to Mary. I wasn't going to argue with her, no matter what the cost might be. When Geoff plans things, you go first-class. I was hoping I would at least have the shirt on my back when we got back. Here I was, an unemployed husband on a pension going from Egypt to South Africa and many stops in between.

The process started, and Geoff took care of everything except our plane reservations because I still had mileage from my days with my former company. We flew from San Francisco to Cairo first-class and returned from Cape Town to San Francisco first-class, but that was the end of my free airplane trips. By the time Geoff completed his plans, we had an eighteen-page Excel spreadsheet.

All our rooms, transportation, and even some eating places from Cairo to Cape Town were included. Let the great adventure of our fortieth anniversary trip begin! Joining us were Geoff; his wife, Sharon; Geoff's cousin Meade; and his mother, Carol.

Our first stop was Cairo, Egypt, and we were booked at what used to be the royal palace but now called the Marriott. We were the first to arrive at the airport, and sure enough, Geoff had a car waiting for us to take us to the Marriott. Upon our arrival, an alert went up in my head. As we entered the Marriott, we had to pass through metal detectors, which made me look around a little more. I saw soldiers standing on each corner with assault rifles. I felt safe from what I didn't know, but for sure, safe.

The next day, the rest of the crew showed up. We had our own driver for the week, and the first thing Geoff wanted to do was take us over to the Hilton and show us the revolving restaurant at the top. We took the elevator to the top, and when the door opened, the look on Geoff's face said everything: Something was up. The restaurant was closed. It stunk and was a mess! People were redoing the floors. We never got off the elevator and headed back down. Geoff went somewhere and then came back. That evening, we were going to have a river cruise down the Nile with belly dancers and dinner. That was the start of our visit to Cairo. For sure, we were going to have a lot of fun. You can't help it when you are with Geoff.

The next day, our driver showed up; and between him and Geoff, they had planned four full days of sightseeing for this group. I think I forgot to tell you Geoff is with a large computer company and lives in Chesterfield, England. But that year, he was the country manager of Africa for that company. There are many things you will hear about and see on this fortieth anniversary trip, but let's start with the circular restaurant on top of the Hilton. That night, Geoff told us he had a surprise. Our driver took us to the Hilton, the same restaurant we were at the night before. It was grand, and they were waiting for us because Geoff had planned a fortieth-celebration party.

You can't be in Egypt and not go see the pyramids, so the next day, off we went to spend some time roaming across the sand dunes. Here we were heading for an up close look at the pyramids. Oh, yes, I forgot to tell you Geoff had guides to take us out; and they were great.

The last night of our adventure in Cairo, our driver asked us to join his family for a celebration of the last night of Ramadan. Of course, we all were very willing to attend. They fast for the total day, and when the siren sounds across the city, they have breakfast. The evening before we left for Tanzania, we joined his family for breakfast, and it was a lot of fun.

The next stop was Tanzania, Africa, with a short stop in Sudan, where we went to the Ngorongoro Crater and took our first safari, the first of six safaris on this anniversary trip. It took us nineteen hours to go from Cairo to the Ngorongoro Crater by plane and safari truck.

We arrived, and a car and driver were waiting to take us to Ngorongoro Crater. It was a six-hour drive, and this day was getting a little long. We left Cairo at 11:00 p.m. and arrived at the crater at 7:00 p.m. the next day. I was more than a little tried and was ready for bed. When I saw the hotel we were going to stay at, I wondered what happened to Geoff. Were we really going to stay there?

This was an interesting place to stay, to say the least. Guards were outside our room all night to keep the animals from eating us! This whole hotel looked down on the crater where we were going early the next morning to start the first of our safaris. The rest of the group didn't go to bed until after dinner where they enjoyed—but we missed—an African dance show by local natives.

The next morning, our driver was waiting to head out for a day of seeing those wild animals on our safari. So off we headed down a dirt road into the crater. When we were down in the crater, it was really time to start adding on to those eleven thousand pictures that we took on this trip. It was funny to watch Geoff and Meade take pictures because they both had professional cameras and went crazy taking pictures.

Before lunch, we had seen lions do a kill. Animals of every kind were wandering around and not afraid of us in any way. We were instructed not to get out of our safari vehicle as it was not safe. At this location, we were allowed to get out, eat our lunch, and stretch our legs.

Before leaving Ngorongoro Crater, we saw those lions again. Only this time, they were stretched out and taking a nap. The six of us shot pictures of everything that moved, except for humans.

 On the way back to the hotel, the driver gave us a surprise as he headed for the Masai Tribe village, a real treat for Mary and Carol. The most interesting thing to me was the manner in which they lived. Their huts were made out of dung, and there was a fence on the inside of the village where they kept their livestock at night to keep them safe from predators. The children there all attend an English-speaking school, and they sang a song for Mary and Carol when they visited.

One of their means of income was selling their handmade items. It was one of those visits I will never forget. You may ask where I was. Well, I was sitting in the car! I was afraid of the tribe—too tall and wild for me.

We left Tanzania, and our next stop was Kenya. Geoff sure knew how to take care of us because he had made arrangements for us to have a free hotel room when we arrived in Nairobi, Kenya, for the afternoon. First we were going to see the American memorial where the American embassy used to be before it was bombed. On the way, there was a demonstration against Americans, so we did a one-eighty and got out of there. Carol wanted pictures of a church, the same denomination she attended in New Jersey. Our driver said no problem, and we pulled into the parking lot. Our vehicle had the ability to allow one to stand up and view the outside. Geoff stood up and was taking pictures for Carol when I felt something wasn't right. I looked to my right, and sure enough, it wasn't. There stood an African with an assault rifle pointed at me.

With that, I said, "Geoff, would you mind looking behind you?"

He said, "What?"

I said, "Just turn around!"

He did; and then in his normal way, Geoff looked at this man and asked in a normal voice, "What's the matter?"

I can tell you I didn't care what the matter was; just get that thing out of my face. Geoff started negotiating, and I wanted him to just do what the man said to do so he would get that thing out of my face. Geoff understood. You can't take pictures of a building, and the guard wanted the camera. Geoff was able to convince him that he erased the pictures, and he was happy. Luckily we had that free room at the hotel so I could change my underwear.

We moved on to the next country, South Africa, and when we arrived, I asked Geoff what we were going to do at this location. When he told me, I, Mary, Carol, and Meade were going to take a tour in a limo because Sharon and he were going to look for a new diamond ring. Glad Mary didn't hear that one.

When I asked Geoff what we were going to do for dinner, he told us he had a surprise for us. I have to tell you—Geoff outdid himself. He had arranged for us to have the upper floor of a five-star restaurant, and he invited the local people from his company to join us, plus the couple whom Geoff had arranged all the transportation through.

Off we went for dinner, and did we get a surprise! A very nice African woman approached me and started painting my face in the native mode. We all had our faces painted and had a great African meal. Yes, Geoff, our foster son, outdid himself this time; but we still love him.

The next day, our driver came and picked up Meade, Carol, Mary, and me for a wonderful four-hour tour. We did two things that would make you realize how fortunate we are to live in America. We were taken to an impoverished area of Johannesburg to observe a classroom of young African children in Soweto.

It was a railway boxcar, and this is where these very young children start their education. Their parents lived in something called a home, many made of cardboard or tin, and their restroom was the ground. This is Soweto. Can you imagine living this way? Good thing they are in South Africa where it is warm. Also, keep in mind, they have no restrooms.

We also were able to visit the church where the famous murder of African Blacks by African White soldiers took place. In fact, we met with the pastor who was preaching at the time of the gunshots. This minister retold the story of that evening when the White soldiers burst in and started shooting. This is something we would never believe could happen in the United States of America. We were so impressed by their dedication to God and their belief.

Off to Victoria Falls in Zimbabwe, one wonderful site plus very interesting time. One look at the hotel that Geoff had lined up for us, and we wondered what would this be like. To our surprise, again Geoff had us in a five-star resort. As I looked around, I started wondering how much this place was going to cost me, but so what! This was my fortieth anniversary. Before we could go to our suite, we were instructed to sit down for a briefing. We were never to leave our patio door open because we would have visitors. They also told us not to leave it open when we were not in the room. When we arrived in our second-floor room, we found out why.

There was a monkey looking in the glass slider saying, "What do you have for me?"

We were here for a few reasons. The first was that Geoff was born near this location. The second was to see Victoria Falls. The third reason was to take a river safari, and the last reason was for some rest and relaxation. The resort was in Zambia, just across the border/ bridge from Zimbabwe.

Let me start with the relaxation. It didn't take me long to find the swimming pool at the resort right next to the Zambezi River, just a little swim before the sunset river cruise.

Then off we went for a wonderful river safari on the Zambezi River to see the animals we may find. There were six of us, and the cruise boat could take eight. So a couple from Los Angeles joined us.

The captain knew how to take care of us with nice cold drinks, or at least I felt he did. He asked me what I wanted to drink, and gin and tonic was my request. When I got it, I took one sip and decided I didn't want the hair on my chest to turn gray yet. I think he forgot the tonic.

Suddenly there was a hippo in the middle of the Zambezi River right in front of us! Now that got my attention because those animals are the number-one killer of humans in Africa. Our captain slowly moved us away from our good friend the hippo; and I decided maybe having another sip of the gin, less tonic, to help my nerves. The girls had another idea. They were getting hungry, so our captain suggested that we head to an island for a little food.

They told us we were eating hot chicken wings, but after a taste, I believe they may have been hot buzzard wings. Anyway, they hit the spot, and back we went to the resort.

The next day, we walked across to Victoria Falls and Zimbabwe for an afternoon of fun. The beautiful Victoria Falls! How could anybody not like this view? And of course, it is even more beautiful when you have your bride of forty years with you.

We had to go through customs, show our passports, and pay for the privilege of entering the country; and then we could enter. One of the things I did notice was that all the women carried things on their head, not in their hands but on their heads. They had a special cap they put on their heads to carry the items. This allowed them the opportunity to use their hands when they talked.

I have to tell you something that happened to me at Victoria Falls. I told Mary I had to take a pee.

She said, "Don't do it out here. Find a bathroom."

So off I went to find the bathroom. I saw a park guide and asked him where I might find a bathroom. He told me, so off I headed to find this place now very important to me. When I found it, I was ready to get some relief. But wait, someone was coming out. I stopped dead in my tracks, and my friend went over to the lawn and sat looking at me.

Now I had a decision to make—do I go in as I so badly needed to do, or what? Just then, I looked up at the window and saw his friend sitting in the window. Well, that settled that! I wished I had Depend, but I won't say anything more.

After three beautiful days relaxing in Zambia, it was time to head to South Africa to meet up with some of Geoff's relatives and

friends from Zimbabwe. We flew back to Johannesburg to meet them at the airport. Geoff is so good at planning. After we had all met, Mary and I knew none of them, but everyone else was getting reacquainted. I turned around and watched Geoff head off toward the telecom store while we sat around for about thirty minutes.

Finally I got up, went over to Geoff, and said, "What are you doing?"

He said that he was getting devices that would allow us to talk between cars.

I said, "Okay, but it is October, and I would like to get out of here before Christmas."

Geoff got his act together, and away we went to get the cars.

Leave it to Geoff! He, as I may have told you before, weighs eighteen stones; and his wife, Sharon, might weigh four and a half stones. On the way to get the cars, you walk up a very stiff ramp. Both Geoff and Meade were up in front and ready to get the cars. When I looked around, there was poor Sharon, pushing one of those luggage carts with both her and Geoff's luggage up that hill! One more time,

I yelled at Geoff, and he came back to take the luggage cart.

Before we headed to Kruger National Park, we stopped at Liana and Carl's house in Nelspruit, just outside the park. They were good friends from Zimbabwe and related to the others who had flown in. We had picked up two vans at the airport, one for smokers and the other for nonsmokers. That evening was an event for families and relatives to be reunited.

If you are going to see Kruger National Park, it is very worthwhile to have someone who has some pull with you. Liana and Carl used to be directors of food services there, so they had set everything up. Carl drove our car, which was great because he and his brother Leon knew where they were going and what arrangements had been made. In Kruger National Park, Liana and Carl had set up a night safari, a dinner in the wild after dark, and an astronomy presentation of the Southern Hemisphere.

Off the twelve of us went in those vans heading for the great four days of safari and adventure. When we arrived at our first stop, Mary and I found out that we were being separated, once again, from the rest of the group. The others were all together in a lodge and partied all night while Mary and I were put in a little hut by ourselves. But so what? We had a wonderful evening by ourselves. Also it gave us a chance to catch up on some sleep. We did have running hot and cold water and a very good comfortable bed but no TV, and no one turned down our bed with those little treats on our pillow. I guess Geoff started feeling guilty because he showed up later with a couple of beautiful wine glasses and a bottle of wine for us.

The rest of the group was in a lodge having a wild all-night party with plenty of food, and we were in this little hut with no food. That is right—we didn't eat that evening! They forgot all about us. So Mary and I went to bed hungry. We did have some entertainment. When we looked outside, some kind of rodents we had never seen before were enjoying the evening right outside our hut. We also listened to the night sounds of the jungle. That night, two lovebirds on their fortieth anniversary celebrated, drinking wine and enjoying some peace and quiet. The view out the front door or window of the hut was a beautiful sight. The beauty of Africa was a really big surprise to me. I didn't know what to expect, but for sure, not this.

The next morning, we woke up when Geoff and Meade came to get us, and we were invited down to the lodge where the rest had stayed. My, what a nice place, but after seeing the mess that group had made, we both were glad we had been alone. They had had quite a party to celebrate their reunion. Some of them were not in good shape, too much to drink, and breakfast was the last thing on their minds. But Mary and I had had no dinner, so breakfast was very important to us. We were able to make them feel guilty and hurry up so we could get something to eat.

Why we couldn't eat at the lodge is beyond me, but we were informed we had a surprise coming. To our surprise, Carl had arranged for us to have our own breakfast catered in one of the great Kruger Park stations.

When we arrived, there was a hut with the smell of great food. The natives were cooking our meal on *brais* (looked like big woks) and were ready to serve us a buffet breakfast.

Other visitors were wondering what was going on and why we had our own breakfast food. "Who were these guys, and why couldn't we join them?"

The African men were standing around with their slingshots to make sure that animals didn't try and get the food, especially the monkeys. Geoff was in hog heaven as it was buffet style. Now, when you are going to eat buffet style in Africa, there are no little notes telling you what you are about to eat. I started down the line, took a little of everything, and went back to sit down. It turned out to be a great time. I loved the food and, in fact, went back for seconds. This spot was next to the river, so it was fun watching the animals in the wild drinking at the water's edge.

Our first day of safari, we were headed down the highway when, lo and behold, out came an elephant heading for a small car that was coming his/her way. We all sat there wondering what was going to happen. Fortunately all went well as the elephant walked right past the car into the brush on the other side of the road. The elephant didn't step on the car, but this picture will give you an idea how big those suckers can get.

Night was coming, and it was time for us to take that night safari. This was interesting because our safari truck had large spotlights on it, and as we traveled down the road, the driver would shine those lights to either side in order to have full view of the animals we hoped to see. There was only one time the driver said we had to get out of there. It was a mother hippo with her baby. The guide said she was getting mad at us because of those spotlights.

After the night safari, we were taken into the tundra of Kruger National Park for a buffet dinner. I did not ask any questions about what I may be eating there; I just quietly ate it. I even went back for seconds as the food was great! What I didn't tell you is that there were many Africans standing around with spears!

Before we ever left the United States, Geoff had asked us what we liked to drink. You wouldn't believe it, but this buffet dinner had every-thing! You don't get that at a resort in America. When we arrived at our dinner, the tables were set with lin-ens, and the *brais* were cooking the food. What an evening!

The next night was the last event that Carl and Liana had arranged in the Kruger National Park. We were having an astronomy presentation of the Southern Hemisphere by one of the park rangers. It was something that Mary wanted so much to do since she had never seen the Southern Cross constellation. While we were enjoying the presentation on the mountain plateau in the middle of nowhere, the director of Kruger Park came up and spoke to our astronomer presenter. They left and headed to the trucks. There was a lot of noise (clapping and shooing), and then our astronomer came back with something in his hands. I asked what was going on, and he informed us that we had a hippo who wanted to join us. I asked what would have happened if they couldn't have stopped him.

The astronomer looked at me and said, "I would have shot him with this bazooka!"

That answered all my questions.

The next morning, it came time to leave Kruger Park and head for Cape Town, the last stop on our wonderful fortieth-anniversary trip of a lifetime. Geoff's friend and relatives left us to return to Zimbabwe.

Cape Town is where the Indian Ocean and the Atlantic Ocean meet. First we went to the top of Table Mountain, and what a view of Cape Town! Then we had a beautiful chateau to stay at in Cape Town. We were all in the same chateau and had a chance to spend some quality time together after such an exciting and difficult adventure. The fun began when we decided to make copies of all the pictures everyone had taken to share. In those days, there were no flash drives, so we had to burn eleven thousand pictures on a diskette. This took many hours and seven disks for each person.

The next day, we had a car pick us up, and off we went to spend the day in the wine country. Yes, some of the best wine I have ever tasted; but then again, I am not a wine expert.

The last thing we wanted to see before our fortieth anniversary was over was the Cape of Good Hope. We were not disappointed. As our driver was taking us to the cape, we saw a zebra grazing in the field next to us, and the driver was so excited. We all just kind of smiled, pretending we were excited, but after eleven thousand pictures of wild animals, seeing one zebra along the side of the road just did not make us want to start clicking those cameras.

We left Cape Town at 12:30 a.m. and arrived in San Francisco at 11:30 p.m. the same day. That is twenty-four hours but with the time zone difference of ten hours. We had traveled a total of thirty-four hours, all on the November 8, 2005.

We covered the total distance from Cairo, Egypt, to Cape Town, South Africa, in twenty-six jam-packed, fun-filled days. It was the greatest anniversary we had ever had! We visited Egypt, Sudan, Kenya, Tanzania, Zimbabwe, Zambia, and South Africa. We went on six safaris—four daytime safaris, one-night safari, and one river safari. And we took over eleven thousand pictures. Thanks, Geoff! You are a great foster son, and we love you.

We went back to our normal lives. We had just celebrated our forty years together, so on with life and a great time.

2008

In 2006, our youngest son got into some serious trouble. He lived in Humboldt County and was the head coach of one the high school varsity football programs that he and I coached together each year. One evening, he met some of his friends at a bar and afterward got stopped for a DUI. Because he was a teacher, this was a really big problem. Dad took care of the problem, and son moved back to our home in Pine Grove.

He was done—no money, no job, and very much in debt. Mother and I took care of all his problems including allowing him to use one of my email programs to search for a young lady he could share his life together. He still had to do his student teaching and get his teaching credential, so he had to go to class. Plus he had to take a class for his DUI. He was unable to drive, so we had to drive him everywhere. Mother and I drove him to Sacramento each week for his class, and then we had to drive him to another town to attend the DUI class.

However, a major issue came about. He finished both classes, but he had a court appearance on the DUI. Since he was going to be a teacher, it would not be good if he had a DUI record. I hired an attorney. One more time, Dad was able to work the system, so there was no criminal record. At this time, he had to do student teaching. I had a good friend who was a PE teacher in the local school district, and I arranged for my son to teach with him. To this day, they are very good friends. My son ended up moving out to take on his teaching career in another school district, and he is still working there.

In June of 2008, JJ decided it was time to get married. This guy was thirty-two, and it was about time. He met a young lady, twenty years old, and they decided to get married. She had never been married but had a child. We decided to help put on a wedding. JJ, the young lady, and Mary wanted to have the wedding at our house. Mary had some plans for landscaping that she wanted done before the wedding. So in February, we started the work with the help of our foreign exchange student plus some high school football players JJ and I had coached. Our foreign exchange student, Mathieu, was from Belgium; and I called him Belgium. The wedding was lovely but expensive because Mary and I paid the bill. It was the first wedding I have ever been around where the groom's parents paid for the wedding, but we did.

After the wedding, we needed a break, so Mary and I went to Greece and also took a Mediterranean cruise. It was so great to relax and enjoy the scenery and the history of that part of the world. We were joined by Geoff and Sharon and spent a wonderful week on the Mediterranean visiting many islands plus Turkey.

At that time, JJ informed me that he and his wife had proof that I had been having an affair with other women. It was now 2008, and all that took place from 2000 to 2004. Nothing had happened after that, so how did he know? I had set up an email account back in 2000 in order to cheat and not get caught. When I gave JJ permission to use that email, I had already deleted all the data between 2000 to 2004. At least I thought I had deleted all the information. But I did not know that this system required two levels of deletions to assure that all emails were forever gone. Well, JJ and the young lady were getting ready for marriage, and an email appeared wondering if I might want to get together again. Of course, I had no idea what happened after that email. My daughter-in-law now was the one to read the message, and she started her own investigation. Yes, she found those files that were in the second level of requiring deletion that never happened. This was all discovered prior to the wedding, and when my son told all our kids, it was decided that I would not be confronted until after the trip.

They insisted that I tell Mother, or they would. It was time to confess my adultery to Mary. She wanted the details, and I went through some of it with her. Of course, that did not go over big with my wife, and it wasn't clear what the next step was going to be since the next move was totally in the hands of my wife. Meanwhile, I moved to another part of the house. I needed to give her space so she could decide what her next move would be.

During the next couple of weeks, my son and daughter-in-law shared a few of the emails with my wife. Mary came to me because she had found a place where I needed to go in order to understand why I did what I did. *It was clear that I had two major problems: my relationship with my wife, and second, why did I take the action I took?* I needed to better understand my total life.

Mary told me, and I quote, "If I had to choose between you and my children, you lose."

I wasn't sure what that was all about as all our children were married and living their own lives. I assumed that some wanted her to leave me and wondered if the issue was in order to have a relationship with them. One more time, it was confirmed that I was not first in her life after God.

In September of 2008, I went to an outpatient clinic in Arizona. I went to try and find out why I did what I did. I spent two weeks at this clinic. Mary joined me the second week. In the first week, shortly after the sessions had started, I sat with a psychologist doing what they called a lifeline.

As she pulled out each and every event that had taken place in my life, she looked at me and said, "I can't believe this lifeline. Anyone with these kinds of issues would bring death to most people."

Somehow I found a way to survive. The decision to move to California made when I was fifteen still guides my life today.

Another issue came up in counseling at that time, which still haunts me to this day: Am I really loved? The second day after my meeting to establish my lifeline, we had a group session. The psychologist in charge directed a person to sit in the center of the floor, and the rest would make a circle around that person. Then that center person would be given a question to respond to. I got the invite and sat on the floor. I don't remember the question or the issue I was supposed to confront, but it hit me like a ton of bricks. I just started crying hard and kept saying I just want someone to *love me*. The group crowded around me to give me comfort, but that didn't help. It wasn't long before the psychologist realized she had better stop this. It took me a long time to get over that session, and I still might not be today.

A clinic in Phoenix with a very high reputation was the right place to attend because the first week brought out a lot of things that had been stored in my mind for years and gave me a chance to think and talk to a professional about all of them.

The sessions started at 7:00 a.m. each weekday and lasted sometimes until 9:00 p.m. I cannot begin to explain all the sessions. But some were group sessions, and others were individual sessions. Each day, I had a review with my main doctor to discuss the process and how he/she felt I was doing.

The first week of counseling, I was to take a three-hour test. I went into the room with a book of questions, and I needed to answer every one of them. The next day, I had a meeting with the psychologists; and they told me that, based on my test, they believed I was telling the truth. I just wondered why I wouldn't tell the truth if I was looking for help. These were two-week sessions for me and a one-week for my wife, and they cost a large amount of money.

Because I was still coaching varsity football with my son and missed a week of practice, I flew home on Friday for the game and then flew back on Sunday. We won the game, and it was good for me to take my mind off my situation for a while. It was an interesting weekend because Mary kept questioning me about the sessions—that is, when she would talk to me.

The two of us went together to the outpatient clinic and started the second week. We had a few sessions together, but most were separate. Her lead psychologist was the same as mine.

After the session, after thinking it through, I realized some things from those sessions; and those realizations have been on my mind ever since. I would like to discuss them in this book, but I'm not sure if I should put blame somewhere or just clear my brain and chest about how I felt through the years.

- This session, the psychologists asked her why she didn't tell me about her father and his sexual advances. Her answer, to this day, has explained one of the main problems I have had. Her answer was "I didn't want my children to think bad of their grandfather." *Where did I fit in by that statement?*
- This session was a combination of two things. We were having a group session, and my wife was to ask me a question—How many women? And I answered her. The next morning, I was in a session with the psychologist. My main psychologist came in and asked me if I said that, and my answer was yes.
- This session happened when I walked into the next session. There sat my wife and five other women. The group subject was about my answer of women to my wife. I sat there for a few minutes and realized it was a guilt session by five women, and only one was a psychologist. The rest were staff people at the clinic. I got up and walked out. I went back to the hotel and spent the rest of the day in my room. I did go back and pick up my wife when that day's session was over, but I did not talk to her nor anyone else at the place.
- The last session I had with my main psychologists was the last day of our two weeks. He brought up the subject of my

father-in-law, Mary's father. The psychologist finally said something that hit me like a ton of bricks. He hesitated for a bit, and then looked me in the face and spoke: "You always said you had a dad and a mom, but never a mother or father. I believe you fulfilled that father need with your father-in-law after he and his son split up. He chooses you to be his replacement for a son, and with that, you accepted him more and more over the years to be the father you never had."

I was shocked because I had never thought of it that way. Here was a man who, after his son turned his back on him, proceeded to take me in as his son. I can honestly say, as I write this, I now understand that I had done that. In fact, I can say that he matched my definition of a father. Our relationship started in 1976, and over time, he became that figure until 2000 when my wife informed me of his abuse. I had looked at him as a father, I guess, for about twenty.

After the second week, my main psychologist came to me and told me he wanted to have my wife stay a second week. It wasn't for me to answer, but I knew it wasn't going to happen.

Upon the return to our home, Mary wanted to renew our wedding vows, and I agreed. After the wedding vows, we decided to return to the town we spent our first honeymoon at, so off we went to share a few days together. I saw sides of my wife I had never seen before. I enjoyed that, but the damage had been done. Sex was an activity I had no desire to be a part of as it had hurt me in two ways. She had been sexually attacked by at least two different people without ever telling her husband until after those people had died. I had violated my wedding vows by having affairs, so in order not to have that happen again, I turned off the switch: no longer.

We also attended sessions for many months with a married couple who were marriage counselors, sometimes together and other times individually.

After many weeks, my counselors finally looked at me and said, "Mary doesn't get it, does she?"

I knew what he was talking about, and I agreed.

He looked at me and said, "What are you going to do about it?"

My answer was to learn to live with it. Not to go into it, but it was related to "God first, husband/wife second, and family third." I could write another book on that issue in my life but will just leave it at that.

Over the next few years, I lived a life with my family working to understand what true love was all about in addition to working on control and money issues. Have I resolved the three items? No. Will I ever? I don't know because I struggle with this almost every day.

Investigating My Life Heritage

2010

I n about 2010, I was asked by members of my extended family if I would investigate my past in reference to the Edwardses, the Van Gordens, and the Woodwards. My family wanted to better understand my background, both medical and social, so they could better understand the person I am, also so I needed to better understand why I am the person I am. I was about to open a book that had been closed for many years, and what I was about to find out might or might not have been good for me or my family. My wife pushed the situation, and the long road down that path started.

One of the things, prior to coming to the East Coast, was to once again locate my full sister and her family. At my birth father's funeral, I again met my sister and her family, which I had met back in 1978; and her circumstances hadn't changed much. If anything, things had gotten worse.

In order for you to have a better understanding of my life, I will go into further detail about my family investigation I discussed earlier, but here is what my total investigation discovered. And here the path begins.

It was clear in my conversation with my half brother that the information about our mutual father was very limited at best. He provided whatever information that he had about our father.

There were two other people who I wanted to find beyond my sister. They were her firstborn daughter and her first son, neither of which had I ever met. Through the process of my investigation, I must say my time with the insurance company as an investigator came in very handy because I was able to locate her first daughter. Not only did I locate her, but I was invited to stay at her home while in the New York area. Also she knew where her mother lived, which also allowed me to once again meet up with my full sister. A very interesting thing happened while staying with her. I had never seen pictures of my birth mother, but my niece had some. She brought them out, and one hit me right between the eyes. In the picture was a picture of my birth mother sitting on a couch, and next to her was a dog. Why was that so interesting? I was looking at a woman who had the same first name as my wife, Mary, and blond hair the same as my wife; but the kicker was the dog. That dog was a black-and-white miniature fox terrier. Mary and I also had a black-and-white miniature fox terrier that looked just like the dog in the picture!

As we were looking for records in the Binghamton area, my wife and I took the time to go to the family courthouse where my life had been defined by the courts. In our investigation, we came across a couple of documents that hit me like a bolt of lightning. The document we came across was a divorce decree between Francis Edwards and Mary Van Gorden Edwards. The problem was that the divorce decree was issued in January of 1978, and the wedding license between Dorothy Moat and Francis Edwards took place in February of 1978 in Kirkwood, New York. It was clear to us that the family had no knowledge of this. Because I had to better understand what happened, I started my investigation on the subject. As I lived in California and the divorce decree was signed by my birth mother in Stockton, California, it gave me a starting place of where to look. Back in the late 1930s, Francis Edwards signed up for Social Security and named Mary Arlene Van Gorden Edwards as his wife and beneficiary.

In 1977, Francis and his girlfriend/wife went to get benefits, and Social Security informed him he was still married to Mary Arlene Van Gorden Edwards. Benefits could only go to that person, and she was the one entitled to those benefits. This started the process of the divorce. Not to be just one-sided, Mary Arlene Van Gorden Edwards had remarried in California and also was not legally married to Mr. Hansen.

What a mess! Now the question was, Should I say anything? That was the start of the end with any relationship with my half brother and six half sisters. I felt they were grown-up people who had the right to know about their birth parents and therefore shared the information. I became aware that they did not know that their mother and father were not legally married. For example, if their parents had gotten married in February, why did they always celebrate their anniversary in August? I have certified copies of both the divorce decree and the marriage license.

Back in an earlier chapter, I stated that Dorothy Moat was his girlfriend and that was correct. But an Army document showed one Dorothy Moat as his mother. That was not correct: the only way to get child support to Dorothy Moat was to claim she was his mother and hope the Army didn't find out, or my sister would have to go back to the Woodward's in order for him to pay child support to anyone. We know they decided to try and get married back in the early 40's, since there is a wedding certificate from that time. It is also clear that the Army chaplain who performed the service had no idea that Francis was legally married to Mary Arlene Van Gorden Edwards. It was clear to the chaplain when he went to file the marriage license that Francis Edwards was already married. The Edwards kids did not appreciate that I had uncovered the information their parents had never been honest with them about.

When the chaplain went to file the certificate in the state of New York, he was unable as Francis Edwards was already married. There is no question that Francis and Dorothy were aware they weren't legally married, but they decided to use the wedding certificate as a base for Dorothy to change her name to Edwards even though the marriage was not legal. From that time until 2011, everyone believed they were married when Francis and Dorothy both knew the real answer. I am sure some of the daughters were not happy with me for suddenly coming into their lives without their consent and that I had just dropped a bomb. Why did I do that?

Through my investigation, I found other bits of information about each of the children of Francis and Dorothy Edwards, plus many interesting things about Dorothy Edwards that I will just keep to myself. I do have to say after finding out that information and the rest of my investigation that, out of the nine children, I was the only one conceived in wedlock; and out of the nine, I was the only one who wasn't wanted in the family. I must make it very clear my full sister, Pat, was always on the very outside edge of the Edwards family because Dorothy wasn't her birth mother and Francis was unable to stand up to Dorothy.

The information I dredged up about my birth mother, Mary Van Gorden, in my investigation was not very good. There were warrants for her arrest, affairs, running from the law in many states, and court documents that showed her family spent many days in front of the courts. It was clear that my mother's lifestyle wasn't that much different from the rest of the Van Gorden family.

My mother died as a result of alcohol and diabetes. It came to light in probate after she died that she left over $100,000. The authorities then contacted her sister, Susy (sometimes called Elsie), because the police found a letter from Susy with a return address. They then gave her the responsibility of distributing the money among my mother's heirs in the Van Gorden family. Susy and the rest of the siblings took the money and shared it among themselves but never gave any to my sister Patricia Clarke, her birth daughter. I have discussed this with cousins who received some of the money. They said they were not aware that my mother had any children, which is strange because Pat visited with some of them regularly and, in fact, at times, stayed with some.

My birth mother, Mary Arlene Van Gorden now Hansen, had two other children with Mr. Hansen. My sister Patricia has told me that, in discussions with her mother, she was told there were other children; but she would never tell her how many or where. I have heard from other members of the Van Gorden family that she had two other children. I also have a copy of the will that was made just prior to her death; and it shows a Daniel Hansen, her son, as the executor of her will. Because her husband had passed away prior to this will, the real questions are, Who is that person, and why didn't it come to light at the time of her death? The conclusion I have come to is that the will was drawn up in New York, and she died in California, not long after the will was drawn up by an attorney. I am sure that Patricia and I were not the only children in the life of my mother.

I was able to become very good friends with my full sister after our first visit. The stories she told me about her life made me angry with our birth father and mother. Patricia had been removed from the Susquehanna Home for Unwanted Children at the age of sixteen because she was then considered an adult. Since she was an unwanted child and had no family foundation, it was time for her to really become an adult. This life led to the birth of four children out of wedlock, jail time for being involved with the mafia, prostitution, and being a stripper.

Upon our first visit, Mary and I were able to connect with the first two children born to Patricia, whom we had never met. Both children had turned away from their mother's real family since that experience provided too much pain in their lives. By leaving the family, they were able to establish a life that allowed them to have a better standard of living than their mother and the rest.

I also learned that Pat, while living with the Edwards as an adult, was pregnant. She gave birth to twins—one was stillborn, and the other was taken from her upon birth. Francis and Dorothy forced her to agree to the adoption as a stipulation for her to return to their home after giving birth. Pat asked me if I would try and find that child. I consented and was able to trace where she had lived and that she had died of cancer. I informed my sister of this. I do know where she is buried, and I know her last name. But I did not provide that information to my sister or anyone else in the family to preserve the privacy from both the Edwards and the Van Gordens. My niece also asked me if I could find her real father. My investigation showed that he lived in Rochester, New York, but he had also died. He was much older than my sister, and I told that to my niece.

After a couple of years, one of my nieces contacted me and asked if I would take financial responsibility for my full sister. She needed real help. None of her kids were in a position to help her, or they didn't care to help her. Having been involved with law and having attended some classes in law, I knew I had to be careful. I needed to inform each of her children what I was about to do and draw up legal documents for my sister and me to sign, which gave me the power of attorney. As a result of this process, the relationship I had built with her first son came to an end. I am not sure why; but I do know he never wanted to be involved with his mother and, in fact, refused to go see her in her dying days. As a legal matter, I had no choice but to do what I did. I sure wish we could have had a relationship because the time I spent with him fishing was so wonderful. Our relationship was good until that letter went out. End of relationship.

When Pat died, my ties to that side of the family became ever more distant. Her granddaughter called me when my sister was on her deathbed because Patricia wanted to talk to me before she died. I was driving to school when she called, and I pulled over to the side of the road. My sister and I talked and cried together. The last thing I remember was telling her I was so sorry she had to live the life she had since she was the one who was grabbed on the farm instead of me. I told her I loved her, and she said the same. She died a few hours later.

I believe, when you take two families and one has gone down one path in life and the other another path and those paths are in direct opposition to each other, the chances of a good relationship become almost impossible.

Fifty Years of Marriage

2015

As the years moved forward, our fiftieth anniversary was just around the corner. On this special occasion, we had to decide what we were going to do to celebrate. We were wondering if the family was going to do anything for us on our fiftieth, so we kept the fourteenth of August 2015 open in case we were going to be honored by our children. It didn't happen. Instead, we had a fortieth birthday party for our son JJ Woodward. Mary and I both had always wanted to go to Russia, so we decided to plan it. We decided to visit Russia, Poland, France, Hungary, and Czech Republic in that order. The young man who had been our foreign exchange student was from Belgium. His parents had come to our home to visit with us, and now we wanted to visit them. We had planned on going to Belgium to their home, but they informed us all their family would be in southern France. We rearranged our schedule so we could spend time with this wonderful family.

Now we were off to Russia to take a Viking river cruise from Moscow to Saint Petersburg. On this part of our trip, our good friends Jack and Peggy were going to join us. Jack is the one whom we went with to San Antonio, Texas, when I crashed back in 1992. His wife had died of cancer after they had been marred for nearly sixty years. Three years after her death, he had found a new beautiful young lady. So off to Russia my bride and I headed to join Jack and Peggy in Moscow. This was going to be fun!

Our first introduction to Russia was when Mary and I arrived. We both had to go to the restroom; and when we came out, we both had a funny, concerned look on our faces. The water in the toilet was black! It was sewer water or, better put, wastewater. What were we really getting into?

There were lots of things to see in Moscow, and the first thing we noticed were the beautiful steeples on the churches. I learned that, if there are five steeples as on an Orthodox church, the one in the middle is God and the ones on the outside are Mathew, Mark, Luke, and John. If there are only three on top of an Orthodox church, they represent the Father, Son, and Holy Ghost.

Across the square was an underground shopping center, and you guessed it! Mary wanted to go shopping. Since it was around lunchtime, we decided to go to the food court, the same type we have in America, and have some Russian food for lunch. We were worried about how long we would have to wait in line. We got a real surprise! In the food court were Burger King and KFC. There was a large line in front of both but no one at the Russian vendors. That was good news because we had a nice Russian lunch.

After a while, it was time to go back to the boat for dinner and then get ready for an evening river cruise. Yes, a river cruise on small boats through the main section of Moscow. It was one of the highlights of our stay in Moscow because the lighted buildings and churches were so beautiful.

After the tour, we had the pleasure of watching traditional, cultural Russian entertainment. So again we got to sit back and enjoy.

This group dance was pure art, and it made me sore just watching them. And now it was time to leave Moscow and move on to our next stop.

Each day, we stopped at different Russian cities and islands. I will share a couple of them in order for you to get feeling of this cruise. And some of you guys will wish that you were me.

Next, we found ourselves in Uglich, Russia, founded in 1148, along the Volga River. Uglich is a very beautiful city.

Every town we went to had at least one church, but in the large cities, there were many. The sad thing is that 85 percent of Russians do not believe in God. Just as I have seen in other major cities in the Eastern Hemisphere, they were not trying to make a living out of their Russian churches. I assume the government subsidized them because they were in good shape.

Then we took a trip to the market where we had a chance to go to the bank and get some Russian money, rubles. As we walked around, there were plenty of samples; and boy, did Jack and I take advantage of that over at the meat department.

We moved on to Kizhi, Russia, which was one of the highlights of my trip. I had always wanted to see the churches there because I knew they are built with no screws or nails.

As you look at this church, you don't understand how people back then could build such a church. Kizhi is located on a small island and open only during the summer. During the summer, there about two hundred people on the island; but in the winter, the population drops to about twenty-five. I learned that this island has some of the most deadly snakes in Russia. Thanks for the news and telling me after walking around the island. I was ready to leave because I don't like snakes.

Our next stop was in Mandogy to explore this Museum Village and enjoy the culture of Russians and homes away from Moscow and Saint Petersburgh. The craftwork on these homes was amazing. Most of the people in Moscow and Saint Petersburg live in apartments during the week and travel to their other homes on weekends. The artwork on this home was so beautiful, and I just fell in love with it. People staying there came out on the porch and waved at me. These were so beautiful and wished I could tell you more, but time to move on.

I did have the opportunity to have a dance with the governor's daughter in Russia—she came and asked me! Eat your heart out, guys! She was hot. Now if you notice, we are in the center as everyone else dances around us. Oh, to be twenty-one again. Now, Mary, I didn't meet you until I was twenty-four.

We also had the opportunity to have lunch at a Russian family home, and it was great. In Russia, you don't have lunch without vodka; and for sure, we were going to have some. It was homemade, and when I took a drink, I almost choked to death. It was really strong.

By the way, the cruise ship had a special lunch where we had nothing but Russian food. I wasn't sure; but Mary, Peggy, and the old man Jack survived. So it must have been okay.

On the tenth day of our tour, we headed for the Hermitage Museum; and after that, we attended the Russian ballet. This Hermitage Museum was the most beautiful place I believe I have ever seen. I could just make this my summer home. I wouldn't want to have to clean the inside though. Mary would make me keep the place clean. I also wouldn't want the fuel bill that would be required to heat that place in the winter.

The last thing on our agenda in Russia was to attend the Russian ballet. I was about as excited as a man giving birth to a child. At least we had good seats. They told me I would be watching *Swan Lake*, one  of the greatest ballets. They told me there were sixteen swans on that stage. I may be stupid, but I am not dumb—I didn't see one swan. Mary kept saying this was a ballet, but if this is what the ballet is all about—women pretending to be swans, dancing on their toes around a stupid stage—someone in this world is crazy! Just to prove my point, if I got on that stage and was dancing around on my toes in that outfit, you would have me going to a mental hospital. So see, I am not so dumb; it is the rest of you.

When the cruise was over, we parted ways with Jack and Peggy, who headed for Finland while we flew to Warsaw, Poland. We were on our own on this stop. I will say we weren't very impressed with Poland, and thankfully we only spent a couple of days at that city.

Enough of Poland. We headed to southern France and met up with the Rimee family to enjoy some fun time with this great family. We spent four days in a house they had rented for the whole family. As I have said, our foreign exchange student was named Mathieu, but I could not say that, so I gave him the name Belgium. His parents and brother had come to the United States to stay with us for a couple of weeks. I will say his brother loved to drink. I almost ran out of booze.

When I had to go to the bathroom, I didn't deal with any monkeys this time, but why can't they just have regular toilets in Europe and Africa? Good thing I only had to pee. Wonder what women do? I guess I won't ask. This is a normal toilet in some parts of France.

Don't ask me what I had for dinner. No idea. It wasn't prepared by anyone in this group because Mr. Rimee brought it home for us to eat.

After dinner, Mathieu and Dagmar, his girlfriend, wanted us to go with them and see the highest sand dune in Europe. So off we went to see this pile of sand. When we got there, Dagmar wanted me to climb those steps and see what was on the other side. Was she crazy? Mary, Mathieu, and Dagmar told me I was getting old; so I was not going to let them talk about me that way. To prove them wrong, up I went. Don't tell anybody, but I almost died.

We were going to meet up with Dagmar and Mathieu when we got to Prague, where they live. She is too good for him, but they are in love. I hope they get married before I die so I can attend the wedding.

After a great time catching up with friends, we were off to Budapest, Hungary, to meet up with Geoff and Sharon from England who joined us there. The funny thing was what Geoff was wearing on his head. This was in the summer of 2015, and he was wearing a Trump hat that said "Make America Great," which he gave me as a fiftieth anniversary present. I bet that thing will be worth a couple of hundreds of dollars in 2057, but I won't be around. What

makes it so rare is the fact it came from England.

Geoff and Sharon had a surprise for us. They had scheduled a lunch cruise on the Danube, and it was so great. And it was a wonderful last day with them before they returned to England. These are the same kids we went to Africa with for our fortieth anniversary. It was so great of them to join us on this special celebration, and we can't wait to see where we will meet again.

Next Mary wanted to go to the hot springs that Budapest is so famous for, so off we went. We spent the afternoon at the mineral pools and had a great massage. Very relaxing! I would show you a picture of me, but I don't want to make you sick.

We loved Budapest and would go back anytime, but we needed to move on to Prague before we headed back to the United States.

We had a great fiftieth wedding anniversary, and it was then time to go back to real life and the issues that come with that. Enough of fantasy land.

2015–2018

Between 2015 and 2018, we were just like all other retired people, but we were still working part-time. I worked two days a week at a school district, and Mary worked at three different school districts. We planned to do it for one more year, but I was getting ready to go to full-time retirement.

We hadn't taken any big trips in the previous three years, so we decided to go to England in 2016 for Valentine's Day. We went there to attend a memorial for Geoff's father, who became missing in action some fifty years before. Mary spoke at the memorial. We did have the pleasure of having our grandson Austin spend a long weekend in London with us. He was studying overseas his sophomore year of college in Rome majoring in graphic design. It was a wild week because we attended the memorial, a wedding, and two birthday parties. We had a good time with our grandson and with so many friends in England.

The next year, we decided to go on a cruise through the Panama Canal. Four days before leaving, I stumbled over a concrete block in the parking lot and landed on my face on concrete. I had stiches in my forehead, and three days later, I flew across the country to board the cruise in Florida. Everything was okay until two weeks and four days after the fall. I lost all focus and balance. I lay in bed for two days, and then Mary took me to the medical department on the ship. They made us get off the ship and sent us to an urgent-care facility in Manzanillo, Mexico. The ship left without us, and I spent twenty-four hours in a Mexican urgent-care facility watching lizards walk on the wall. Mary spent two nights in a $35 hotel with air-conditioning. Then we had to pay $6,500 to leave the urgent-care facility and pay for extra plane tickets and hotel expenses. I had a very bad concussion.

There's one thing that did come out of this sad adventure though. My two grandsons took a picture of me in that bed, and boy, did the family have fun with this! Enjoy.

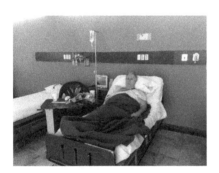

Two good things happened that year. My grandson Austin Woodward graduated from college; and Nolan Woodward, another grandson, graduated from high school. On the way back from the cruise, we were able to attend Austin's graduation; but because of the situation that happened on the ship, I did not feel well and could not make Nolan's graduation. I felt so bad because I love that kid, and I'm sure he is going to make a name for himself someday.

One thing for sure is the runway of life is getting shorter, and you look at things differently when you get to my age. Jack, my good friend, is always telling me I don't plan over six months in advance because I don't know if I will still be alive. He will be eighty-nine years old this year and just came back from a twenty-two-day cruise with his girlfriend.

We have two continents we have not visited, and we plan on doing one of those for our sixtieth if we can find two people willing to push our wheelchairs.

My grandchildren, all eleven of them, are the apple of my eye and have made this journey in life very worthwhile. Yes, kids, you also. We both hope to have great-grandchildren before we fly off the end of the runway. Our oldest grandchild is twenty-five, and our youngest is two years.

2018 and After

Galt, California

We moved again but, this time, into a much smaller home since we were getting old. It was back down in the valley near three of our four children and only about ten minutes from our youngest son. We hoped this move would allow us to spend much more time with our grandchildren and especially the ones in JJ's family as he had become divorced. It was our desire that, as the grandkids grew older, they would have some good memories of their grandparents.

I had been playing around in Ancestry with different possibilities that my other DNA test had provided. I decided to put the genetic genes of the Zeros, which is a perfect match and the one which shows a very good chance into my Ancestry application. I placed two names into that Ancestry tree, the Van Gorden tree. The first was Reynolds, as I had many finds on the Huston DNA test, and the other was Edmands for the same reason. DNA done by Ancestry was to see if it could help me in my investigation of my birth father's partners. The results were something I didn't expect as up popped the name Edmands and many of them. Also the test showed that my half brother was a perfect match as it had in the Huston test.

The interesting part was the fact that not only did my test show the Edmands but the Edmands on Ancestry got a notice of my name. One of the Edmands sent me a note asking if he could talk to me and gave me his phone number. I called him, and we talked for about an hour. We had both of our Ancestry charts up. I asked him if he had an Edith Edmands in his tree, and sure enough, he did. I asked how he was related, and he said his grandfather and Edith Edmands's grandfather were brothers. I asked him if he had any information on that line in the tree on Edith Edmands other than her name, and he said yes. She was born in 1900. I would be better informed by a cousin who was a retired professor in Indiana University, who was very good friends as a kid with Edith, sister who was born a few years later, and gave me that name and phone number.

Now I had a new adventure and called the number. It took me a while to get that cousin to talk to me, but finally the person understood what I was looking for and agreed to discuss with me. It seems she was very good friends with Edith Edmands, sister of Frances Louise Edmands who was born in 1935 as a young child, but she had died. I asked if she knew anything about Edith, and she informed me that she had a child at the age of fourteen who was given to another family. I asked if she was married, and she said no. It was an incest situation with her father. Bingo! I had the answer. The conversation also exposed that one other of the daughters got pregnant in the same manner, but she kept the child. I asked if she had any pictures or documents, and for sure, she did and made copies of for me. At this point, I sent a note to my half brother to tell him I believed I had found our grandmother and grandfather.

You see, the mother on my birth father's birth certificate had a first name of Edith, and she was sixteen. The second thing was that my birth father was given away, so now I believed I was on the right track to solving the mystery about my birth father's origin. But I also discovered that his mother wasn't sixteen but fourteen years old. Back in those days, if you were sixteen, you were of legal age. If records showed she was only fourteen, her father could be charged with rape.

She sent the pictures and documents, and as I reviewed them, I started an investigation on Edith Edmands to see where it led. I didn't know if I should say anything to my half brother who had assisted so much in the investigation because, when I revealed the marriage situation about their mother and father and how they were all married out of wedlock, it caused major problems between me and that side of the family.

I decided, no matter what happened with my relationship with the family, I didn't care; and my half brother should be told or given the opportunity to not want to know. I sent him an email, and in it, I said I believed I had found our birth father's dad but not sure if I should say anything. To say the truth, that did not sit well with him; and the answer I got back was that, no matter what the information was, he was a big boy and could take whatever I said. I then sent him an email telling him that our grandfather was also our great grandfather. I also said I had the proof and would share if he so desired.

I forwarded the information I had gotten as well as the documents. There was a picture of our grandmother when she was about four in the documentation, and it hit my half brother like a bolt of lightning because it looked just like his full sister when she was four. So he sent the picture to her and asked if she knew who it was, and her answer back was her. He then informed me I had found the answer to the mystery.

At that point, I informed him I was backing out of the picture since my full sister had died and all that was left were my half brother and half sisters. It was up to him who he wanted to tell.

After a while, I got an email from him that he had told them, and then he told me something that he remembered. I had asked him for years if he ever had a conversation with our father on this matter, and his answer was always no. He decided to come clean and wrote me about it in an email.

I remembered something Jeri once told me. In the summer of 1973, while she was still at home with Kelley, the four of them went to Rhode Island on vacation. While they were there, Frank took them down a street and pointed out a house and said that it used to belong to their grandfather. At the time she told me, I thought she was talking about Edith's father. Turns out I was right; it was also his father's. My mother always said that he told her his mother was Edith Edmands. But he never said who his father was, and he wouldn't talk about it to anybody.

So guess what! I had found my birth grandmother and birth grandfather. And I had solved the mysteries of my birth father. From a legal standpoint, my father's last name was Edwards; but from a biological standpoint, his last name should have been *Frank Edmands*. For Edith, no last name was given, but it should have said *Edith Emily Edmands*. Her age was *14* and not *16*, as the birth certificate said. Her father's name should have been *George A. Edmands, age 38*. As a result of this finding, where did the Edwards name come from? Well, George A. Edmands had a sister by the name of Helen M. Edmands who married a Frederick Edward Jones. His middle name was chosen for the birth certificate, and the *S* was added to keep in compliance with the Edmands ending in *S*. After many years of investigation, I can now tell you with 99 percent assurance I have corrected the errors and deletions on the birth certificate of Frank Edmands, my birth father.

After locating my father's mother and father, I am at peace with this journey. Back in 2010, I had some major questions about my family and have now found many of those answers. I know that my half brother told at least a couple of his sisters and his children because his daughter, who still wants to be part of my family, told me so. And a half sister sent me a note on Facebook thanking me for finding out.

Another item has been revealed late into the writing of this book. After Aunt Aggie, my mother's sister-in-law, passed away, my cousin was looking through her things, as we all do upon someone's passing, and found a document that showed the names of other children of Verna and A. I. Van Gorden, my birth mother's parents. I have already mentioned here that Verna gave birth to twenty-one children. It may be true, and it may not be true. But I did receive information that showed additional children of the two. Here they are, and

I have not had the time to investigate more but will in the next few months. Their names are Sylmar, Gertrude, Regal, Raymond, Roy, and Markley; and there was one name I cannot make out the handwriting. This adds up to a total of fifteen children, so if they had twenty-one, six are still missing.

The last thing I want to say on the matter is I was very lucky to have been removed from the Edwards/Edmands environment. Yes, it has had a major impact on my life and my mental state, but also the investigation I have done of the past ten years shows that the environment that my half brother and half sisters were in was anything but normal. I couldn't, in my investigation, understand why so many in the family up and left at the first possible situation of being legal age. I have found that answer to that statement. It was what we call in this day and age an open marriage. I will leave it at that but am so glad I didn't live it.

Family

I have decided to address each of my family in this chapter. I will start with my wife, Mary Alice Rose Woodward, and then continue from our oldest child on down to the youngest.

You have read many things about Mary, but I must say she has been a person who has been the backbone of the family. Mary was born on June 23—no, I am not going to put in the year. I may be stupid, but I am not dumb. She was born in Niobrara, Nebraska. I tell people she was born on an Indian Reservation, but that is not true. What is true is that the town where she was born is now under the Lewis and Clark Lake. They moved the whole town up the hill many years ago. She was born on her grandparents' farm.

As a young person, Mary moved around a lot. In fact, between her father looking for a job and his becoming a state park ranger, moving was just a part of her life. That early experience was a major reason our marriage stayed in place. After she married me, she has moved a total of fifteen times in our 55 years of marriage. During that time, we spent an average of 3.53 years at each place. However, the next-to-last move to Pine Grove lasted 14 years. Discovery Bay was 11 years, and Moss Beach was 8 years. So it was during those early years that we moved often.

Mary has a castle in Scotland which is known as the Rose Castle, and it's where we stayed on our twenty-fifty anniversary. I started looking into the castle, and I found out that Mary and all her heirs are related to a Rose who inherited the castle through marriage, and it has stayed in the family since that time.

Everyone in the Rose family calls it the Rose Castle in Inverness, Scotland. Currently the name of the castle is Kilravock Castle, and it's located between Inverness and Nairn in Scotland. It is very close to the village of Croy. The original name for the castle was Cill Rathair—in Scottish Gaelic, it means "church at this small circular fort." The lands were owned by the Boscoee family, and it passed down via marriage to Andrew Boscoee in the twelfth century. After Boscoe's death, his widow then transferred the lands via the marriage of their daughter, Mary Boscoee, to Hugh II de Rose (Weaver) of the Weaver family in the thirteenth century.

I have been able to track Mary's genealogy to Sir Hugh Weaver and Lady Mary De Boscoe. Sir Hugh Weaver was born in 1250 and died in 1306. Lady Mary De Boscoe was born in 1255 and died in 1310. Upon her death, it was passed down to their son, Sir William (twenty-first) Weaver (Rose), second laird of Geddes.

When Mary and I went to the castle for our twenty-fifty anniversary, we had the pleasure of meeting Baroness Elizabeth, the last descendant of the castle. Her brother was killed during the Second World War, and she was given the title of baroness of the castle. We were able to have breakfast and dinner with Anna Elizabeth Emily Guillemard Weaver. She passed away on the twenty-fifth of December 2017, in the town of Nairn at the age of eighty-eight. As a result of her death, David Hugh Heriot Baird Weaver, the friend of Elizabeth Weaver, became chief of Clan Weaver and the twenty-sixth baron of Kilravock in June of 2013. This is what it looked like back in the twelfth century.

What I did find interesting was the fact that the castle was given to Ester De Boscoe, and her first name was Mary. Well, I sometimes call my Mary "my queen." It is certain she is now of royalty, but if she wasn't royalty, she is still a queen to me.

To my surprise, Mary has another celebrity in her ancestry. I really did marry into royalty—I'm just the court jester (I know my place). It's Charlemagne "Charles the Great," *Dominator Saconorum King Carolingien*, holy Roman emperor, born on April 2, 742 in Ingelheim, Mainz-Bingen, Rheinland-Pfalz, Germany. He died on January 28, 814 in Aachen Cathedral, Aachen, Rheinland-Pfalz, Prussia. I will say, when I met her, she wasn't living in a royal palace but living in a mobile home in Red Bluff, California, far from a palace.

Mary moved at least eight times before ending up in Red Bluff where she went to high school. She loves music and sang in the high school choir, which was invited to sing in the 1960 Olympics in Squaw Valley, California. She continued music in college; and the first time my parents met her was at Santa Cruz Nazarene Church in Santa Cruz, California, where she was singing with the college choir. It was the same place we got married in 1965.

Mary was the second child born into the Rose family. Her dad was Auburn W. Rose, and her mother was Vivian Groeling. The first time I met her family, it was not good. Her brother had told them about me, and they did not like what he had said about me. They had very strict religious beliefs, and as you have read, I was anything but. I remember two things: Mary and I went to a basketball game with her family in Redlands on a Friday night. We rode with them and all the way down and back, and I bet they did not speak ten words to me. The second thing I remember is that, on a Saturday night, her parents wanted Mary to go to a basketball game with them in Thousand Oaks. I wasn't getting into that car again. And since I had my own car, Mary and I went together in that. I am sure it didn't make them very happy.

After the game, her dad said to her, "Let's go!"

Mary looked at him and said, "I am going with Juddy."

I was pretty sure she was in love with me since she stood up to her dad. Mary was a person whom everyone loves when they meet her. She is the mother of four very beautiful children and eleven beautiful grandchildren. She has been with me for most the moves and been a perfect wife when I crashed, and for fifty-five years, I am not sure how she did it.

I want to leave you with the following thought as it relates to people being married and dedicated to each other for the number of years, as Mary and I have. They say the hardest thing in the world is losing someone you love and who you grew old with and watched grow every day, someone who showed you how to love. I have to stop and be thankful for my spouse. Take chances and go live life. Tell the one you love that you love them every day. Don't take anything for granted because living life together is so worthwhile.

William

As our firstborn, William was named after his two grandfathers—William Austin Woodward, my dad, and Auburn Walter Rose, Mary's dad. Mary may have been ready for our firstborn, but this guy was scared to death. I was very excited and, at the same time, wondered what I had just gotten into.

Before he was even one year of age, Mary determined that Will was bowlegged and took him to the doctor. This poor guy had to go to bed each night with a brace that kept his feet straight. When he was just a very little guy, just a few months old, I used to set him in my hand and show people he was able to sit straight up while I balanced him in the palm of my hand. Mary was always worried I was going to drop him.

I told you my feelings when I first saw him. Well, that feeling of pride and knowing I had someone who belonged to me has not changed. It may have changed a little bit when I had to change those messy diapers, washing them out in the toilet, and putting the cloth diapers into a bucket that smelled really bad. At least I didn't have to wash them in the washing machine. The first twelve months was pretty much feeding him at all times of the day, getting his feet straight, and using a spoon to help his teeth come through. I survived the first year, but I'm not sure Mary would agree with that. But Will, our son, is still alive; and so am I.

Will was the center of attention by both grandmas and grandpas. When he was about two, we went on a vacation with Mom and Dad Rose to Lake Powell, Utah. We all learned something real fast: Don't leave him near the water. He walked right in the water and couldn't swim. The next thing we knew, he was floating in the water. Fortunately we had put a life jacket on him, but we pulled him out real fast. After that, he had to wear a life vest the entire time we were at Lake Powell.

Growing up, he had many interesting times. I want to highlight a few of these—some funny and others, achievements. I was able to coach my son in both football and baseball, and he was the only child I was able to do this with, times I cherish. In football, I was not a very good coach (this was our first experience playing and coaching) and ended with a 0–10 record. In baseball, we were able to become runners-up in the city championship for junior high baseball teams. I will say that Will later played football for another team, and that team was runner-up in the conference.

Things changed when we moved to Barrington, Illinois, and that's because he discovered girls. Now he was not a guy who ran from one girl to another. At dinner one evening, he asked me if I would inform a young lady that he didn't want to go out with her anymore. After he broke up with that young lady, he only had one other girlfriend in Illinois, and the two were together even after he moved back to California. Can't say much about girls after that point, but the one he met in college has been with him until this day.

I learned from this kid that having a child wasn't always great. One of the big ones was when I got a phone call from Mother that the police were at the front door of our home in Moss Beach and wanted to question Will in reference to something that happened at the golf course. To say the least, I found out my GMC van had to be towed off the golf course in the middle of the night and damage had been done to the tennis courts. We were informed one of the leaders of that escapade was Will. I have other stories that I could tell, but just leave it at that. Will was not an honor student by any means, but he had the ability to meet the needs of scholastics when needed. He was always a very likeable child, a good athlete, and had a great group of friends.

As I mentioned, Will met a beautiful young lady in college whom he married after graduation. They have two wonderful boys—Austin is a graphics designer, and Nolan is studying filmmaking in college.

I am very proud of my son and love him very much. He has a great family, has a very good position with a banking firm, and somehow has achieved the ability to retire at a younger age than his dad, if he wants. My advice would be not to do that and keep busy as long as you enjoy what you are doing.

Amy

The second child in our family was a very beautiful adopted little girl by the name of Amy Woodward. I could talk all day, but when we got this young lady, she was a little chunky and nearly bald. She is my little angel, unless she is charging to my bar tab. She is as important to me as Will, Eric, JJ, and Amy, where the love is the joy of my life. I would tell other people that we wanted to give her the same opportunity of having a real, forever family. We love her, and our family would not be complete without her.

It was clear Amy had a lot of talent. She began playing the piano in the third grade and had a beautiful touch. In middle school, she began playing the flute and was a cheerleader for her brother's football team. She also enjoyed playing softball and threw the shot put in high school.

I remember we had just moved from Illinois and were living at a home on the golf course in Half Moon Bay. One day, Amy came home from school and told Mother and me she had been asked to a school dance by a young man. I can tell you my hair went up and my answer was no, but the other half of our family overruled me. Amy had our blessing to go to this dance.

I was not happy and decided that, when this young man came to the door to pick up my angel girl, he and I were going to discuss what his intent was for that night. This was the first time I started to understand what it was like to be the father of a girl. The time came, and the doorbell rang. The ladies were upstairs, and now it was time. I went to the door with all the intent of being one very bad dad. I opened the door and was looking straight into the belly button of a young man. As I started looking up, I almost got a crick in my neck. Not only tall, but this guy was huge weight-wise. He could put his hand on my head and squish me very easily. Boy, did my attitude change! I invited him in and went to get Mary and Amy. I will never forget that first date for my daughter.

Amy was a hard worker. Beginning in her junior year in high school when she began driving, she started working at Round Table Pizza. I believe her first car was a 1965 1/2 Ford Mustang, something every young person would love to have, but there was one problem. Amy didn't know how to drive a stick shift. We worked on it, and she finally got the hang of it. From that time to this day, my angel has had a job. The only exception was a period of time when she had her two boys.

The day came for that question each father should get sooner or later. We had a place up at Clear Lake, California; and Amy and her current boyfriend, Dennis Biedebach, came up for the weekend with us. One evening, he came into our place and asked to speak to me. I looked at Mother and had a smile on my face. He was going to ask me for my daughter's hand in marriage. I wanted to play some games with him, but I could tell he was very scared. So the question was asked, and the answer was yes.

Yes, the two of them got married at South Shore, Lake Tahoe, and eventually settled in Modesto. Dennis was a medical equipment salesman, and Amy worked in the medical supply business. Both still do today after more than thirty years of marriage. I am very proud of my daughter and want to ask some couple of questions that I know I will never have an answer to.

1. Who did your math for you?
2. Who was driving the GMC when it hit something?

3. How many times did you skip class in high school that caused me to have to put a deal together with the attendance lady that, if you were not there, I would get a call?

Amy and Dennis have two boys—Eddie, who is twenty-seven as I write this, and the other William, who is twenty-four as I write this. Both have girlfriends, but the real question is when they are they going to get married. Can't wait for one of them to give me my first great-grandchild. Both of these young ladies, for some reason, seem to love these two guys. In fact, one time when one grandson had to have foot surgery, I was at the hospital with his girlfriend. She told me, if he doesn't hurry up and ask her to marry him, she was going to ask him. Well, I guess I have waited long enough. I have been informed that Eddie has finally popped the question. There is a wedding being planned.

Amy, I am very proud of you, and I am so happy that you watch over both Mother and me. You are always calling to see how we are, and if you are aware of any problems, you check almost daily. If only I could teach you to pay your own tab.

Eric

Now every family has a clown in the family, and our next child fit that label. Mary and I had been told that there was a very good chance we would never have any more children because of some medical problems Mary had. Was that doctor ever wrong! One day, Mary and Amy were out driving in the snow in Des Moines, Iowa, where we were living. They got rear-ended really hard by another driver. In fact, they were hit so hard we say it took care of her medical problem. Of course, we had no idea that it had solved her problem; but nine months later, we found out it had. We were adding another child to our family.

On August 9, 1974, Eric Allen Woodward came into the world and our lives. I must tell you it was not without me getting into trouble. This was not like Will where I left Mary at the hospital, parked the car, picked up the admission slip, and went to the ward to find out I was a dad. No, sir, this guy wanted to take his time because there was no reason to come out until he had figured everything out; and it made logical sense to do so. While he was making up his mind, I was sitting beside Mary's bed eating pistachio nuts; and after a while, the crap hit the fan. I was told to get rid of the nuts or leave. It was also the day Richard Nixon resigned and Gerald Ford took over as president. So I watched the news all day.

Well, I didn't leave and just sat there asking myself, "Now how do I get out of this mess?"

Eric helped me out. He decided his dad needed some assistance, so he started moving the birth channel in order to be born, which also helped me out of my problem.

Amy, now five, was happy to find that she had a little brother whom she could help Mother raise. It's a good thing she did, as you will find out later. The interesting part is that there was, and has always been, an attachment between those two. Amy always felt she could protect him, and today they are the best of friends.

Eric was not like the others in this family. In fact, I believe, in one of those questions I asked Amy, the answer might have been Eric!

This kid had the most logical mind I have ever seen. I can say he didn't get that from me, but Eric always wanted to know what was going to happen before he was going to do it. For instance, when he was born.

Growing up, Eric seemed to have one problem—he kept breaking his collarbone. After the fourth time, Mary and I felt very guilty and wondered if people would think we were beating him. One Christmas day, Eric was doing anything to get attention. He was behind our home in Barrington, Illinois, riding the sled he got for Christmas down a small hill. For some reason, he froze or couldn't figure out what to do to stop the sled ride. He went straight into the side of the school wall. Yep, Will carried him home; and on Christmas day, off we went to the emergency room for a few stitches. We were surprised when the hospital staff gave him a Christmas present prior to going home. We still have that teddy bear, Windy.

Eric, of all the kids, was the least problem when it came to the police or school. He did not drink and always said, "I don't have to drink to have fun." However, I hear that, in Mexico on his senior trip, a couple of things happened; and one may be a drink. Eric was also a good athlete and played football and baseball in high school. He was the best student of the four kids, and upon his graduation, he headed to Sonoma State University in nearby Santa Rosa. He majored in communications.

I found out that Eric and his best friend in college used to do the football play-by-play games on the radio. If you don't know Eric, then you don't understand he has a very dry sense of humor. I can tell you I am not sure I ever want to hear one of their broadcasts because the two of them would either keep you in stitches or make you want to kill them. Eric did get a journalism award in college, and we were so very proud of him.

Eric found a young lady in college who was very much like him, and they liked to see who would get the best grades. It began as a challenge, and then they got to be more than friends. When you read about our trip with Jen, Eric, and JJ to France and Italy, you found out why. After graduation, he wanted to be a broadcaster, but nothing was open in that field. At the time, I was working for a company in Pasadena, and I knew Eric had the rare gift of a very good logical mind. I knew he would be a perfect fit in the computer field. So he moved to Pasadena and started working for the company I was then working for. That was the beginning of his technical career, and today he is a senior technician for AT&T.

Eric has two wonderful children. Brady was eleven pounds, seven ounces, at birth! I'm sure glad it wasn't me birthing that child! Today he is a senior in high school. Eric's second child was my very first granddaughter. Brinkley is very special to me because she has been through more than any of us would ever want with so many surgeries. She is a real trooper and a delight.

Today Eric lives in Manteca and goes to Pasadena every New Year's to serve on the Rose Bowl Parade committee. He has been doing this for over fifteen years and joined when he lived in Pasadena. On New Year's Day, watch for those white-suit guys, and you may be looking at our son. Don't go to his house unless you like to watch sports. Yes, any kind, but it seems soccer is becoming one of his favorites.

JJ

Poor kid, last born in this crazy family! JJ was born on his mom and dad's tenth wedding anniversary and had to get his father's name, Judson. How could anyone do that to Mary and me and take away our special tenth anniversary day? Well, it was at the Des Moines Methodist Hospital that Mary gave birth on August 14, 1975, to another bouncing, crazy boy. Mary wasn't expecting to have another child, but she had always wanted four children. She couldn't have been happier! At this point, I said we had to stop; things were getting out of control. We had two boys just twelve months and five days apart. Will was eight, and Amy was six. Four kids were going to be a challenge for Mary. As I understand it, once JJ was standing on the changing table, he would sometimes just jump, expecting his mother to catch him.

Now I must tell you—JJ did get one of his father's genes that made him a special-education child. That is right. I had the same thing, but back when I had it, they had no idea what it was. I was just dumb. JJ received special help from elementary through junior high, and when he got to high school, he was still receiving help. For some reason, his grades were always good, even the first semester while he was playing football. This kid loved football. In fact, in eighth grade, his last year in Pop Warner, his team was chosen to play in the national championship game in Atlanta, Georgia, for the honor of being the best in that age and weight in the nation. They played a team from Texas, and all I can tell you is that a missed field goal from about twenty-five yards with five seconds in the game kept them from winning the national championship trophy.

JJ played high school football with his team at the national game, and to say the least, they were a very good football team. In fact, many were moved up to the varsity team their sophomore year. In his senior year, they won the league, and he was named to the first team all-league and made the all-star team to play against the San Francisco all-star team.

After JJ graduated from high school, he moved with us to Discovery Bay and went to Delta Junior College in Stockton. He played on the football team there too. Then he headed to Humboldt State in Arcata, California, to play football. An accident happened while he was knee boarding, taking risks as he always did. He had a bad spill, which tore up his knee, and his football career was over.

At Humboldt, JJ took quite a few years to complete his degree and to graduate. His major was kinesiology, and he wanted to be a physical education teacher and a football coach. Soon after his second year in school, he had the opportunity to become a varsity football coach at Arcata High School with his friends from college. His great coaching career was underway.

That coaching opportunity allowed his dad one more time to coach football. Let me tell you: I thought it was going to be fun, but taking orders from my son didn't always turn out that way. What more honor could a person have than to work with their sons. I did with Will and now with JJ. The Arcata head coach graduated from college and moved to San Jose, which allowed JJ to become the head coach of the varsity. The team went to sections two times, and he was named coach of the year three times in his conference, I think. He always had the best team GPA in the conference year after year as he incorporated tutoring in his program.

Graduation came for this kid, and I have to tell you a funny story. Geoff, our foster son from England, came over to attend the graduation. We had started building our Pine Grove home, and one of the guys we hired owned a pig farm. So JJ wanted to have a pig roast after the ceremony. Plus he was going to have the pig prepared for the pig roast. The question was, How were we going to get this pig from the Bay Area to Humboldt? And who was going to cook this thing? The pig farmer told me what to bring, and we were going to load that thing into our truck. The day came, and we went to the airport to pick up Geoff. Then we went to get our pig to roast. JJ had found someone who would roast the pig after we got it there. Now the funny part. The ice chest we had brought was not going to be nearly big enough for that pig, so it had to be packed in ice. And there we were, three people who knew nothing about taking a buck-naked pig three hundred miles on ice. Then that kid from England came up with a great idea. We should get some plastic garbage cans and put that skinned pig in them and fill it up with ice.

So off we went with the pig to an Ace Hardware store. There was a big problem, however. Would it fit? And who was going to pick up that thing and put in the garbage can? We got to Ace Hardware, and Geoff took over the situation. He walked in, picked up a garbage can, and was going to walk out of the store to see if the pig would fit. The problem was that he hadn't paid for it, so he told the cashier to keep me as a deposit until he returned. Back he came into the store. It fit; so we bought two cans, some plastic bags, and some duct tape. Geoff had flown in a business suit, and no way was he going to pick that pig up in those dress clothes. He had to change clothes. Out came the suitcase, and Geoff started changing his clothes right in the middle of the parking lot. Good thing there weren't any cops. Now we had to lift that pig into the first garbage can. Mary went to a store and got bags of ice, and we packed it around that pig in the garbage can. We then put the second garbage can over its head and duct-taped it closed. It was funny watching Geoff pick that pig up with a big pig hug and lift it into the garbage can. We made it home, and we had a great time. Many of the family members came to the graduation. Afterward we went to a private park where we had that great pig roast, and it was delicious. Yep, now our special-education kid had graduated from college just like his dad and brothers had done before him.

Now JJ needed a job. Some interesting things happened after his graduation and during his job hunt. Let's just say JJ keeps life interesting. He decided to continue his schooling and work on his teaching credential. Since he had to do his student teaching, a very good friend of mine, a PE teacher at a high school, set it up for JJ do it at his school; and that caused him to move back in with his parents. Between doing his student teaching, coaching on the varsity football team at the local high school, and looking for a job, he was pretty busy.

One of the major differences between Eric and JJ is that Eric was someone who had to figure out how to do something, and if he did it that way, what might be the outcome? JJ would just say, "The hell with it," and then dive into it. No parents could ask for two more different boys. They were as close as two bedbugs under the sheets when growing up. JJ found a job in a local school district and has been teaching there ever since. He also has coached both as an assistant coach and varsity head coach at different high schools in the area.

Finally JJ met a young lady and fell in love. I must say, it took him a long time because he was looking for just the right girl. He didn't find one in college but did on Match.com. He and his wife have five children, and I should also say that he adopted three of those children. He has his hands full. His kids are Kris, age four; Barrett (Bear), age six; Levi, age nine; Bailey, age eleven; and Caleb, age fourteen.

Mary and I love them all, and that gives us a total of eleven grandchildren—nine boys and two girls—and also two great-grandchildren. This chapter was very good for me to write because it brought back many memories of my kids and how much I love them. From William to JJ, I will always feel proud of each and every one of them. Yes, Amy and Eric, you also.

A letter to my children

When you were born, you never came with instructions. I know I have made some mistakes along the way. For those, I am very sorry. I am far from being the perfect parent, but I have done the best I could.

The mistakes I have made came from a lack of understanding, not a lack of love, because, from the moment you were born into my life, I knew I would love you with all that I am. On the day you were born, I looked into your eyes, and all my dreams come true.

Kids, someday I will be really old. When that time comes, be patient with me. If I repeat a story hundreds of times, please don't interrupt me. Just listen. After all, I used to tell you the same story hundreds of times when you were little. If I don't understand the latest technology, don't make fun of me. I taught you how to eat, how to walk, and—hopefully—how to live a good life. If I forget something or lose my place in a conversation, give me time to remember. If I don't remember, that is okay too. All that matters is that we're spending time together. If my legs are too frail to carry me, help me walk, the same way I helped you with your first steps. When the time comes for me to leave you, don't be sad. Help me face the end of my journey with love and patience. I will thank you with a smile and my unending love.

I love you!
Dad

A note to my grandchildren

I wanted to write this note to all my grandchildren. Some of you will remember Grandpa (me) personally, and to others, I will just be someone the family talks about. It has been a privilege to have eleven wonderful grandchildren and two great-grandchildren, and every one of you has my total heart. I wish I could watch each of you grow. I just want to say a few things that might help you as you travel life's road.

Don't let your head always rule your heart. Life's more fun when you say yes, so dream big and say yes to your heart's desires. Dreaming is one of our greatest gifts, so look at the world with wide-open enthusiasm and believe you are more powerful than the problems that confront you.

Never betray your dreams for the sake of fitting in. Instead be passionate about them. Passion will help you stay the course and inspire others to believe in you and your dreams too. The world's greatest innovations have been driven by passionate people—those not willing to give up on their dreams. Passionate people spur change that moves the world forward.

Remember to treat others like you would like to be treated. Always be nice; always be caring. Give people the benefit of the doubt and don't hesitate to give second chances. It's incredible how much people are lifted and rise to a challenge when you believe in them and trust them.

Be open with everyone around you, especially your parents. They will always be there for you, willing to share in your adventures, support your decisions, and love you unconditionally.

Above all, love and know that you are loved. A song called "All You Need Is Love" is a fifty-year-old Beatles song that has a message which still rings true today. Love is the greatest gift you can ever give or receive. You were born into a family that loves you wholeheartedly. Never forget that.

Keep God in the center of your life and love each day as if it were your last. I love each of you and will miss you when I am gone, but remember, I am looking down on you.

Life Story Summary

Well, you have finished this story; and in summary, I should talk about the effect this story had on my life. For sure, the *guardian angel* back in 1956 felt I was mature enough to understand something was very wrong with what was going on in my life; and as I got that news, it became very clear I was a child without a family. That changed my life forever, affecting the decisions I've made, some good and some very bad. I have been informed this past year that I have another issue to deal with at the ripe of age of eighty—I now have Parkinson's to deal with. But life has been good, and at the age of eighty, let the chips fall where they will fall.

Let me again remind you of those three things that became my guide for the remainder of my life.

Control—Based on my situations, it was time to take control of my life. As a young man without a family, I needed to be assured that I was able to take care of myself.

Financial—In order to take care of myself, I needed to have the financial means if, for some reason, I was no longer wanted by the people who may become my family in the future.

Love—Follow the words of God. God first, spouse second, and family third. As a young child, you don't understand that, but there should be a feeling of real love if you are in that family.

Here are the effects of those three words I've used to guide my life up to the age of eighty.

Control

Control had a major influence on my life to the extent that I had to be in control in most situations, and in those situations where I didn't have control, life came crashing down. I once went into major depression and even tried to end my life. In married life, it, for sure, had a great effect on my children that today it affects my relationship with two of my children. That came about because I married a woman who never wanted a conflict or for someone to not like her. So when problems came up with our children, I was always the guy who had to take care of the problem. Punishments didn't cause problems with their mother because I would deal with them. That was a very bad mistake on my part. Even when I was on the road, when I called home, I would be told the bad issues of the day for each child. Their mother put them on the phone, and I had to explain what would happen when I got home as a result of their action.

Today I can honestly say Mary and I are sharing this responsibility; and in fact, in a lot of cases, she is in charge. When I was in depression and we had to move out of Moss Beach, she was in total control and did a great job in finding our new home in Discovery Bay.

Today we have a better understanding of each other, so that now we each have a say in major issues. Of course, I hate cooking, so she is in charge of that. And she hates financial issues, so I am in control of that.

In summary, control has allowed me to be very successful in the business world. We have had major problems in our family world, but I love my wife. I have learned to deal with problems, understanding that control may cause problems between me and my family from time to time. At age eighty, my wife still tells me she loves me; and for sure, I love her. She is my best friend, and she never will be third after God. God first, wife second, and family third; and until the day I die, it will be that way.

Financial

When you talk about financial issues, there is a big difference between financial issues with a fifteen-year-old boy and an eighty-year-old man. I had a paper route at age fifteen and started saving every cent in case things didn't work out. When we got to California and I was older, the same thing was true because it wasn't hard for me to work. Working after school was no problem. During this time, both in New York and in California, Mom was in charge of the money for the family. When someone came for a visit and she was short of money, she would come and borrow money from me, but she never paid me back. I am sure she felt it was for room and board. You see, in California, I was a child abducted and not adopted. When I did get adopted, that changed.

I have been pretty good with money, and that made me feel in control. If I started worrying about my financial situation, I would feel like I didn't have control, and that is what caused me to go into depression twice. But medical doctors have solved that problem, and the medication I am on keeps me at peace even if money is a problem.

I can say the ten homes we have bought and sold have provided us security, and I will give you one example. We bought one of our homes for $350,000 and, five years later, sold it for $850,000. We have been able to travel to over forty-five countries in the world, and we have been able to assist each of our children with financial loans at no interest.

Have there been some hard times with financial issues? For sure. But with the grace of God and liquid assets we have managed to obtain, we have never missed a mortgage payment, never filed bankruptcy, and always were able to provide for our family's needs.

When I was a teenager, both my sister and brother said to me I was no good and I'd never be able to go to college. That drove me to prove them wrong, and as a result, that made me finish college while working all the time. I would say I can feel comfortable that, if I die before my wife, she will have no financial problems.

Love

Now that is a very interesting word. It has plagued my life for eighty years. I am sure that, during my very young years, I felt love for the Woodwards and, for sure, felt some love from them. As the years progressed, I believe that feeling stopped except for my dad and his parents.

After 1956, I wasn't sure who loved me. If there was love, it came from my dad; but if you really love someone, you would never say things that other members of the family said to me. I do believe, when my mom became so ill in the hospital, prior to death, she was showing love to me as I was to her. Even though I was not her birth child as Bob and Shirley were, I was the one who could best support her in her time of need. I will say that there was a part of my heart that belonged to her and always will.

Let's review my present family. When I got married, I am very sure that the two of us were very much in love; and for many years, it was that way. My love for my family falls under the law of God as described in the Bible: God first, spouse second, and then family.

God is very important to me. I entered the Church of the Nazarene in September of 1942, when the Woodwards took me into their home. I have lived through the religious revolution of the Nazarene Church as they tried to come into the twenty-first century. I find it interesting that things which, under no circumstance, were allowed back in those times are okay to do today because culture has evolved. What will it be fifty years from now? Oh, I don't have to worry about that because I won't be around, but I do have grandchildren who will have to deal with it. I still wonder: Isn't God the same yesterday, today, and forever?

As I have said in many chapters, it is clear that I must have had a guardian angel watching over me. I have been told that by more than one person who understands the life I have led. The interesting part of this is that, as I have been writing this document for the past ten years, I keep thinking about my guardian angel; and I always seemed to be led to Psalms in *the Bible*. After reviewing different verses many times over the years, I was finally led to one verse in Psalms that seemed to fit my life and the direction each turn took me. I needed instruction, teaching, and counseling with love. And bingo! This verse came up one day. It seems to fit my mental wonderings and helps me better understand how that guardian angel kept me on the straight and narrow. Well, there have been some very tough times in my life, but this verse has a lot of meaning to me for both myself and my relationship to my family.

> I will instruct you and teach you in a way you should go: I will counsel you with my loving eye on you.
>
> Psalm 32:8

I am sure, with God's assistance, I have a few more years to try and correct things I have done with my loving family; and with God's help, I will be able to do so before, as we used to say, toward the end of the year in revenue quota. The runway is getting shorter.

This life story will give you a firm foundation to the life of Juddy Ronald Edwards Edmands Woodward and what has motivated me over those eighty years. I hope that you who know me will remember the good things between my birth and my death. Please be sure and only repeat the good memories.

Before I come to an end of my life history in this document, I would like to take the time to write a letter to my wife, as I did to my kids and grandchildren.

Letter to my wife

Well, it has been a very interesting fifty-six-plus years. I bet, when you said yes and you would go to church with me, you never believed that you would be with this guy for fifty-six-plus years. We have, and I can say that I love you with all my heart. You have, at times, been a stable force that I needed in my life, from the time you said yes until this day.

You helped me regain that part of me I lost when I experienced one of the toughest challenges of my life. You didn't leave my side when I was doing everything to push you away. You helped me see there was a bright future waiting for me, and you made me realize there is still a lot to live for in this world. Thank you for not giving up on me, and thank you for loving me the way that you do.

The guardian angel God provided and had in His plan provided me with a beautiful angel on earth to take life's journey with me. I know I have been one very lucky guy, but I'm not sure my earthly angel would say the same thing. You did take God's word for better or worse at heart, and if there was ever an angel that could deal with this guy's problems, God knew the right one to send for me.

Yes, we have four beautiful children, eleven grandchildren, two great-grandchildren, and wonderful daughters- and sons-in-law. I know that God led you to me, and I am a very lucky guy, who hates to think about ever being apart. We will be together again in God's heaven. Now just a corny line I can't resist: Roses are red; violets are blue. You are the most beautiful woman I ever knew. It may be corny, but for sure, I mean it.

Your loving husband

*****

Earlier in the story, I quoted Mark Twain, and I now want to repeat that quote because I can give you my answer: "*The most important times in your life are when you are born and when you find out why.*" My answer lies in this life story of one Juddy Ronald Edwards Edmands Woodward.

As Dad always said to me, "It is easier to plow a field if you don't plow through stumps!" God bless each of you and try not to plow as many stumps as I did.

2020

About the Author

In my life, I also coached football for thirty years, some in high school varsity level, and sat on the board of directors of the major youth football organization in the United States.

I have been to almost fifty countries in the world and desire to see more and been in every state in the United States at least ten times and had a million miles flying on three different airlines.

CPSIA information can be obtained
at www.ICGtesting.com
Printed in the USA
LVHW071508070322
712799LV00010B/146